Why I-CARE & Why I-CARE Too

Donna and Ashley Ivey

Copyright © 2024 Donna & Ashley Ivey

All rights reserved.

ISBN: 9798320135410

DEDICATION

To all those whose voices I've sought to amplify, whose stories I've endeavored to share, and whose causes I've tirelessly championed, this book is dedicated to you. As a daughter, sister, wife, mother, and grandmother, I celebrate whatever stage in your life represents the best you ever. Your resilience, courage, and determination inspire me every day. I dedicate everything who I am and aspire to be and become to my children and grandchildren. Thank you for allowing me the privilege to stand alongside you in the pursuit of love, resilience, and tenacity in your advocacy in your careers and life today and tomorrow. May our collective efforts continue to create positive change in the world. *Donna Ivey*

To my children Angela and Kevin, I love you dearly. I am so proud and grateful to be your mom. Your births are a continuous reminder to me that miracles happen. Mommy loves you ♥ *Ashley Ivey*.

CONTENTS

Foreword 1
Preface 3
   Part 1: Donna's Story 3
   Chapter 1: The Roots of Care 3
   Chapter 2: Early Aspirations to Advocacy 3
   Chapter 3: God's Strategic Plan Continues to Unfold 4
   Chapter 4: Navigating the Storm 4
   Part 2: Ashley's Story 4
   Introduction 4
   Chapter 5: Beyond the Diagnosis 4
   Finding Strength in Struggle 4
   Chapter 6: MS 5
   Chapter 8: Secret Sauce #1 5
   Chapter 9: Secret Sauce #2 5
   Chapter 10: Secret Sauce #3 5
   Chapter 11: Secret Sauce #4 6
   Chapter 12: Secret Sauce #5 6
Part One 7
Donna's Story 7
Introduction 8
   Who I Am Today 9
   Care Advocate Renovate Educate 10
Chapter 1: The Roots of Care 12
   Self-Care Lessons from Childhood 12
   Case Studies & Essential Self-Care Tips 14

- Essential Self-Care Tip #1. Prioritize Your Physical Health 15
- Essential Self-Care Tip #2. Embrace Emotional Well-being 16
- Essential Self-Care Tip #3. Set Boundaries 19
- Essential Self-Care Tip #4. Engage in Self-reflection & Personal Rejuvenation Activities 21
- Essential Self-Care Tip #5. Cultivate a Support System 23

Chapter 2: Early Aspirations to Advocacy 25
- Donna's Youthful Dive into Healthcare 25
- From Curiosity to Career: My STEM Journey Begins 25
- Empowering Your Path in Healthcare 28
- Five Essential Insights for Aspiring Medical Professionals 28
- Navigating Life's Detours: Embracing Change and Perseverance 29
- Five Guiding Principles for Navigating Life's Changes 30
- Health Care Administrative Experience 32
- Where I Learned the Importance of Having an Advocate 32

Chapter 3: God's Strategic Plan Continues to Unfold 35
- Entrepreneurship, Family, and Faith 35
- The Miracle of a Closed Door 36
- Family Incorporation into the Business 37

Chapter 4: Navigating the Storm 39
- The Dual Role of Family Caregiver and Advocate 39
- The Initial Shock and Role Realization 39
- Accessibility Checklist 41
- Blending Family Caregiving with Advocacy 44
- Navigating Ashley's Journey 44
- Self-Quiz: Are You a Family Caregiver, an Advocate, or Both? 44

Our Journey with Ashley and Multiple Sclerosis 46

Closing Thoughts 51

Part Two.. 52

Ashley's Story 52

Introduction... 53

Early Beginnings.. 53

Faith, Family, Strive for Excellence, I-CARE 53

Chapter 5: Beyond the Diagnosis 58

Finding Strength in Struggle 58

Triple Insight: Navigating Healthcare from Every Angle... 59

Living with Grace: A Journey of Poetry and Resilience Through MS.. 60

Chapter 6: MS 62

The Unraveling of Normal 63

To Be Me.. 65

My First MS Symptoms... 67

Reshaping of My Life 69

School & Graduation 70

Social Life 71

Family Life... 74

Conclusion 77

Chapter 7: My Secret Sauce 79

Chapter 8: Secret Sauce #1... 81

Positive Mindset: How Thoughts Transform Experiences... 81

Chapter 9: Secret Sauce #2... 84

Embracing Vitality: Harnessing Fitness and Nutrition in MS Care...... 84

Movement: The Foundation of Recovery......................... 84

Five Personal Strategies for Staying Active 86
Nutrition: The Foundation of Wellness 87
Key Insights on Mindful Eating When on Medications 89
Understanding Emotional vs. Physical Hunger 89
The Role of Whole Foods 89
Experimentation and Flexibility 89
Hydration 89
Listening to My Body 90
The Synergy of Movement and Nutrition 90

Chapter 10: Secret Sauce #3 91
Treatment: Navigating the Maze of Healing 91
Having A Goal 92
Finding A Hobby 93
Cooking 93
Gardening 94
Self-Healing Nature of Service 96
Treatment: Medication 96
Finding Equilibrium 99
Steps To a Balanced Treatment Plan 99
Walk Away from the Game 100
Walk Away from the Game 102

Chapter 11: Secret Sauce #4 104
Having an advocate 104
Someone to speak for you when you cannot 104
Positive People 105

Chapter 12: Secret Sauce #5 107

Faith, the Unseen Anchor in My Journey 107
MS Relapse, My Faith & My Right Hand.. 108
Tears 110
A Poem by Ashley Ivey 110
The Cycle of Faith & Advocacy Continues 112
Vision 113
A Poem by Ashley Ivey 113

Foreword

As I reflect on my life's path and my mother's, I am struck by how faith, advocacy, and perseverance have shaped our journey. "Why I-CARE and Why I-CARE Too" is a narrative that explores my life and my mother's, mainly through the lens of my battle with Multiple Sclerosis and her unwavering role as an advocate. This is your invitation to explore the depths of our experiences, where personal challenges catalyze profound transformations and where the inception of our family business, I-CARE Inc., became an integral part of our individual lives.

Founded in 1993, I-CARE Inc. provides family-focused, quality nursing and personal care services for clients of all ages in the comfort of their homes or our residential assisted living home, I CARE Homes. It was established long before my health took an unforeseen turn. My early involvement in the business since age 14 played a pivotal role in my life, especially when I was diagnosed with MS at 18. This was instrumental in accessing Medicare coverage for my medical expenses and provided my parents with the flexibility needed for my care. My mother, Donna M. Ivey, emerged not just as a parent but as a fierce advocate, a role she mastered before my diagnosis but became crucial in our fight against the disease.

In this book, we share our experiences and the wisdom of being both a caregiver and a care recipient. Our goal is to reach families navigating similar paths, offering strategies to become effective advocates for their loved ones. Advocacy in healthcare is more than dedication; it requires knowledge, persistence, and an understanding of the healthcare system, a lesson my mother learned early and applied throughout our journey.

My mother has been a tireless advocate for me and countless others, navigating the complexities of healthcare and personal adversity. Her journey, from her youth in Toledo, Ohio, to becoming the backbone of I-CARE, is a testament to her commitment to caregiving and advocacy. This book is as much her story as it is mine. It highlights the importance of advocacy in healthcare – a mission she embarked upon long before I was diagnosed with MS but one that became profoundly personal and instrumental in our battle against the disease.

As you delve into these pages, you will discover the challenges we faced and my "secret sauce"—the combination of factors that has seen me through 20 years post-diagnosis and lead to a fulfilling life. This secret sauce includes having a strong advocate like my mother, who navigated the complexities of healthcare and ensured the best possible care; a mindset shift and perseverance, believing firmly in overcoming challenges regardless of the odds; and a balanced treatment plan that includes medical and mental health strategies.

Preface

Part 1: Donna's Story

Chapter 1: The Roots of Care
Self-Care Lessons from Childhood

This chapter chronicles Donna from a childhood marked by financial adversity in a resilient family to her passionate advocacy for wellness. It outlines how these formative years laid the foundation for empathy, self-reliance, and a deep-seated understanding of the importance of self-care. Through Donna's personal experiences and reflective case studies, the chapter offers vital strategies for wellness and advocacy, stressing the need for a harmonious balance between looking after oneself and caring for others, all presented with practical guidance and spiritual reflections.

Chapter 2: Early Aspirations to Advocacy
Donna's Youthful Dive into Healthcare

This chapter explores Donna's initial interest in STEM and her journey toward becoming a passionate advocate in the healthcare field. It discusses her health struggles and the leadership roles that inspired her to pursue her advocacy goals. Through her experiences and life lessons, Donna offers practical advice for those seeking a career in medicine and strategies for overcoming obstacles. The chapter demonstrates how early curiosity and challenges can be transformative, guiding aspiring medical professionals toward impactful advocacy in the healthcare industry.

Chapter 3: God's Strategic Plan Continues to Unfold
Entrepreneurship, Family, and Faith

Donna's journey as an entrepreneur, merges with her dedication to family and a deep faith, revealing a path directed by divine guidance. She demonstrates the powerful connection between professional pursuits and personal advocacy. Driven by her daughter's healthcare needs, Donna sheds light on how integrating her children into the business, strategic insurance planning, and steadfast support from their church community shows the synergy of faith, family, and business in overcoming challenges.

Chapter 4: Navigating the Storm
The Dual Role of Family Caregiver and Advocate

Donna delves into the profound journey of navigating the responsibilities of caregiving and advocacy within the family. She addresses the initial shock and the gradual acceptance of these roles, emphasizing the delicate balance between personal affection and the necessity for objective decision-making. Through poignant case studies and personal reflections, the chapter reveals the complexities of caring for a loved one with chronic illness, the evolution of a caregiver into an advocate, and the indispensable role of support systems. Donna shares her insights on adapting to these roles effectively, underscored by her own experience with her daughter's health challenges, illustrating the transformative power of combining love with advocacy in the quest for healing.

Part 2: Ashley's Story

Introduction

Ashley describes growing up in a Christian household, reflecting on her mom's start of I-CARE and how it became a big part of their lives. These early years laid the foundation of her faith and extraordinary work ethic, preparing her for what was to come.

Chapter 5: Beyond the Diagnosis
Finding Strength in Struggle

Transitioning into her own story, Ashley shares her struggle following her diagnosis and the effect it would have on her life. She provides practical insights and encouragement for anyone dealing with a debilitating disease. Drawing from her personal experience, Ashley offers a guide to navigating the labyrinth of the healthcare system and the importance of having an advocate who can speak on your behalf when you can't.

Chapter 6: MS
Two Letters That Were the Turning Point in My Life

"Diagnosis Day- It was a day like any other, except it wasn't. Twenty years ago, sitting in a sterile doctor's office, I, Ashley, on the precipice of adulthood, was about to hear two letters that would redefine my existence." Sharing her innermost fears and feelings upon hearing her diagnosis for the first time, Ashley talks about what it was like to realize that everything she had planned for her future was about to change.

Chapter 7: My Secret Sauce

Ashley talks about her life filled with highs, lows, trials, and triumphs, as well as how she endured countless treatments and medications and read tons of books and articles to pursue her path toward wellness. Reflecting on two decades of learning to live with MS, she shares her recipe for overcoming the physical and mental challenges she faced. "It's not the result of a single miraculous remedy, a secret treatment unveiled," she said. Her "Secret Sauce," a blend of lifestyle choices, mind shifts, and personal philosophies, enabled her to emerge victorious.

Chapter 8: Secret Sauce #1

In this chapter, Ashley reveals how changing your mindset and thoughts can transform experiences. This allowed her to accept the "new normal" and transform challenges into achievable goals. "Believing that obstacles can be overcome has made tackling them far more manageable," she said.

Chapter 9: Secret Sauce #2
Embracing Vitality: Harnessing Fitness and Nutrition in MS Care

This chapter focuses on the crucial roles of physical activity and mindful eating in managing MS. It explains how having a consistent exercise routine and a balanced diet can help improve physical wellness, enhance the quality of life, and promote recovery. Ashley describes her continuous quest to maintain and enhance her mobility with MS.

Chapter 10: Secret Sauce #3
Treatment: Navigating the Maze of Healing

This chapter guides readers through the complexities of multiple sclerosis (MS) treatment options, emphasizing the importance of informed decision-making and finding the right balance in healthcare. "Recognizing that mental stress can trigger MS relapses and, exacerbate the illness. I discovered the importance of engaging in activities that alleviate stress."

Chapter 11: Secret Sauce #4

Having an advocate: Someone to speak for you when you cannot.

This chapter highlights advocacy's crucial role in helping individuals navigate the healthcare system. It emphasizes the significance of having someone who can support and champion your needs when you are most vulnerable. This ensures that your voice is heard and your best interests are always considered.

Chapter 12: Secret Sauce #5

Faith: The Unseen Anchor in My Journey

In this chapter, Ashley explores the significant influence faith has played in managing her MS. She discusses how spiritual beliefs and practices provide support, solace, and optimism, which are essential in navigating the challenges and victories of coping with a chronic illness.

Part One

Donna's Story

Introduction

As I sit here, my heart brimming with emotions and eyes glistening with tears, I find myself at the cusp of unveiling a narrative deeply etched into the core of my being. This book, a labor of love and a testament to resilience, is not just a collection of memories; it's a mosaic of life-changing experiences, each resonating with God's grace and guidance.

The process of penning down my story has been cathartic, filled with moments of introspection and revelation. It strikes me now more than ever how profoundly I have been blessed by God's unyielding presence in my life. Each challenge I faced, every tear I shed, and the joys I encountered were divinely orchestrated, shaping me to be an instrument of His will, to stand firmly in the gap for those engulfed in the shadows of hurt, disappointment, or despair.

This book chronicles my life's path, marked by humble beginnings and profound lessons in advocacy and resilience. It traces my evolution from a young girl shouldering responsibility in Toledo, Ohio, to a mother and advocate navigating my daughter Ashley's MS diagnosis. Each chapter of my life contributed to a deeper understanding of care and advocacy, shaping my purpose and direction in ways I could never have anticipated.

Within these pages, you'll discover how life's unexpected challenges can be the most transformative. My experiences, both caring for Ashley and facing my early struggles, have been instrumental in molding my approach to advocacy and support. This narrative is not just about establishing a healthcare initiative; it's a heartfelt exploration of how personal trials and triumphs can unveil one's true calling.

Join me on this intimate journey through moments of joy, sorrow, strength, and perseverance. It's a story that highlights the power of standing up for those who need a voice, whether it be family, friends, or those we encounter along the way. In sharing my story, I hope to inspire others to see the potential for growth and impact in every life experience, particularly the most challenging ones. "Why me?" is a question that often lingers in the minds of those who encounter life's storms. Yet, during this time, I have learned to embrace these storms as divine appointments, each one a steppingstone to a greater purpose, a broader horizon. My experiences are not solely my own; they are a reservoir of lessons and insights meant to be shared, offer solace, ignite courage, and remind us of the profound strength that lies in faith and perseverance.

Who I Am Today

To set a framework for my story, it is proper for me to introduce to you who I am today. My name is Donna, and I am the owner and founder of I-CARE ® Inc. I started my company in 1993, driven by a compassionate desire to meet the healthcare needs of people of all ages.

In the first 15 years, I-CARE focused on rehabilitation staffing services, building a robust team of over 80 therapists specializing in physical, occupational, and speech therapy. We quickly became the go-to for staffing in Northern Virginia's home care and facility sectors. This period laid the foundation for I-CARE's ethos and reputation as a leader in healthcare services.

Recognizing the need for more comprehensive care, I-CARE evolved its services into hourly nursing and personal care. Our team, now nearly 100 strong, spans registered nurses, licensed practical nurses, licensed certified nurse aides, and personal care aides.

Our primary goal at I-CARE has always been to foster the safety and independence of clients with diverse health needs. Our dedicated team of nurses and caregivers offers comprehensive care across multiple settings - clients' homes, hospitals, assisted living, or independent living facilities. We're committed to providing our clients the support they need wherever they consider home. The range of services our caregivers provide is extensive, covering all aspects of daily living. This includes assistance with personal hygiene and bathing, meal preparation, dressing, managing incontinence, and engaging in recreational activities. Our caregivers offer companionship, perform light housekeeping duties, and provide safety reminders. These services are all tailored to help our clients live comfortably and with dignity in their preferred environment. By focusing on these critical aspects of care, we ensure our clients can age in place gracefully and receive the compassionate support they deserve.

Over the 30 years of providing this care and meeting with hundreds of families, I was inspired to expand and enrich the array of services we offer to the public. I dream of capturing the complete picture of what our clients and clients' families want and need. 1993, when I started my company, I-CARE was created as an acronym for I-Care About Restoring Excellence in Healthcare. We humbly marched in our mission statement, requiring high standards for our nursing and nurse aide team. We led in the healthcare technology movement in the early 2000s, initiating a paperless note system that both helped efficiencies and ensured the security of patient information. We fostered and implemented a patient-centered approach to care, where transparency of patient information and collaborative decision-making are intricately involved with their progress. This empowers individuals to actively participate in their healthcare and cultivates a sense of shared responsibility, ensuring that every step is taken with the patient's well-being and informed consent at its core.

Tony, my husband and co-owner of I-CARE, brings a unique dimension to our services with his background in construction engineering. In the early 2000s, he began offering home modification management services, a crucial aspect of ensuring our clients' living spaces are safe and conducive to their needs. His expertise has been instrumental in transforming homes into more accessible and secure environments for our clients.

His work involves managing various projects tailored to each client's specific requirements. This includes the installation of grab bars in critical areas to prevent falls, stair lifts to aid mobility between floors, and even comprehensive room remodels to accommodate medical equipment or mobility aids. Additionally, Tony oversees door-widening projects, essential for clients who use wheelchairs or walkers, ensuring they can move freely and safely within their homes. These modifications are vital in allowing our clients to safely and comfortably remain in their homes. By addressing these crucial aspects of home safety, Tony's contributions significantly enhance our ability to provide holistic care that extends beyond medical needs, encompassing our clients' overall well-being and independence.

Care Advocate Renovate Educate

Our growth over three decades is encapsulated in our expanded mission of Care, Advocate, Renovate, and Educate, echoing our commitment to holistic care and addressing the varied needs of our clients. At the heart of our approach is patient empowerment. Advocacy for transparency and collaborative decision-making has been a cornerstone, enabling clients to actively participate in their healthcare. Drawing on my four decades of professional and personal healthcare experience, I was a knowledgeable patient rights advocate. Clients who required assistance in understanding and navigating the healthcare system brought me on board as an essential part of their healthcare team. I was the intermediator or translator of sorts, their expedient guide through the labyrinth of misinformation, convoluted medical terminology, intricacies of health insurance, and various obstacles that obstructed individuals from accessing top-notch, clear-cut care. I found resources, created solutions, and resolved the most challenging of situations. My secret to my client's success was my experience. Drawing on four decades of healthcare expertise, I possess the foresight to discern clients' needs, preempt potential challenges, and stay ahead of the curve, ensuring a proactive and unparalleled approach to every facet of their well-being. This commitment to education and empowerment led us to establish training programs for personal care aides and certified nurse aides, where we instill core values of compassion and patient-centric care.

Reflecting on this fills me with gratitude for the opportunity to make a tangible difference in people's lives. 'Why I-CARE' is not just my narrative or a chronicle of a business's evolution; it's a testament to faith, resilience, and an unwavering commitment to care. Now that I have covered who I am, it is important to share how I came to be. My experiences in life shaped my existence; the struggles I have witnessed, endured, and overcame have gifted me with important insights that continue to build my foundation of faith. Loving what I do is a gift; loving people is a joy, and I am grateful for every lesson I have learned in this process called life.

Hello, I am Donna Ivey. Welcome to 'Why I-CARE.'

Chapter 1

The Roots of Care

Self-Care Lessons from Childhood

> "Trust in the LORD with all thine heart; and lean not unto thine own understanding. In all thy ways acknowledge him, and he shall direct thy paths." - Proverbs 3:5-6, The Bible, King James Version

My story takes place in the lively heart of Toledo, Ohio, a city teeming with activity but also marked by the harsh realities of struggle. I was born into a close-knit family of five girls, each of us only a year apart. We grew up in a world of modest beginnings and financial limitations. Our childhood was not the picture-perfect one that many dream of, but it was ours, filled with fun, laughter, and a bond that only siblings so close in age could share. We were a unit, inseparable in mischief and growth, and we had no idea of a life beyond our neighborhood. I am the second of five daughters born to my parents. I was born in Milwaukee, Wisconsin, in 1963. Within three years, we moved to Toledo, Ohio, in 1968 and stayed with family until my parents rented an apartment they could afford in Toledo's inner city. The area was plagued by poverty and had many unfortunate characteristics. However, as a young girl, I knew nothing of a world outside my own, and I thought that was how everyone lived.

It was here, amid the modesty and challenges of our family life, that the seeds of my passion for advocacy and caring for others began to take root. Around 1971, my parents divorced when I was only eight. My mother, a symbol of resilience and strength, took on the immense responsibility of raising us all by herself. She worked tirelessly as both a full-time single mother and the sole provider for our family. My mother's unwavering commitment and perseverance in the face of adversity became my earliest lesson in determination and sacrifice. She wore every hat imaginable. "She worked full-time as a paralegal, cooked for us, provided for our needs, ensured that we were clean, and taught us how to present ourselves well. Despite being a single mother of five girls, all of us being a year or less apart in age, she managed to do it all. I can't even imagine what she went through, but I understood at a young age that I was there to help her in any way I could. Being the second oldest made me grow up quickly, and I felt compelled to support my mother and my younger sisters. It wasn't a "duty" or a "chore"; it just was. I learned from my mom how to braid hair, and then I took on the role of hair braider for my younger sisters. One by one, I would part their hair, comb, moisturize, and braid it for my sister. My mother also taught me to balance a checkbook and pay bills at age 12. I then took on the role of treasurer at our home, ensuring bills were paid and needs accounted for. From the simple act of braiding hair to managing household finances, every task carried a weight far beyond its surface. These were not mere chores but vital life skills, each shaping my understanding of empathy, support, and the profound impact of caring for others. The responsibility I was given of taking care of my younger sisters and our household not only developed my maternal nature but also honed my financial skills, making me savvy in navigating the intricacies of managing a home. It was a formative experience that nurtured my caregiving instincts and equipped me with the practical skills to ensure the well-being of those entrusted to my care.

As I took care of my family, I learned the importance of taking care of myself. When I was around nine years old, I had gotten a splinter deep in my foot from walking around our apartment with no shoes on. Despite the sharp, seizing pain, I chose to keep silent and not tell my mother. Though I was young, I understood the delicate balance she had to play with our finances and didn't want her to have to spend money taking me to the emergency room. The pain was sharp, yet my silence was sharper, a conscious decision to shield my mother from additional financial burdens. The pain was intense and non-relenting, and it stifled my ability to help my sisters and participate in the necessary chores around the house. It was then I realized that not taking care of myself hurts others. The injury I did not seek help for caused additional strain on our family as it hindered my ability to contribute to our household actively.

I eventually told my mother about the splinter, and she took me to the emergency room to have it removed. By the time it was removed, the wound was no longer superficial; it had logged much deeper into my foot. This experience profoundly reaffirmed the importance of self-care, a concept that would later become integral to my approach to healthcare.

Caretakers must prioritize their health; prolonging getting the help you need makes the injury to yourself worse and makes you an inefficient caretaker.

This incident sparked my young mind to aspire to get into the medical field. I wanted to help people and myself in a time of need.

Case Studies & Essential Self-Care Tips

Taking care of ourselves is not just important, it's essential, especially when we are responsible for the well-being of others. In my roles in the healthcare field, both in administration and as a hands-on clinician and caregiver, I've seen firsthand the consequences when family caregivers neglect their own health while tending to a loved one. This oversight can lead to a decline in their health, sometimes with tragic results. To illustrate this point, I'll share some anonymized real-life examples from my professional experience. Each story is a reminder of why self-care is not a luxury but a necessity for caregivers.

After presenting these examples, I will introduce one of the five essential self-care tips I've developed and found effective. These tips are not just theories; they are practical strategies that have proven critical for maintaining the delicate balance between caring for others and oneself. As someone who has been in a caregiver's role, struggling at times with prioritizing my own needs while caring for my daughter Ashley, I understand the challenges involved. These strategies have worked for me and many others in similar situations, underscoring the importance of self-care in caregiving.

Case Story #1

In a case that we encountered at I-CARE Inc. a patient was suffering from a severe, life-altering illness. His wife, deeply dedicated to his care, had been his primary caregiver for many years. She was involved in every aspect of his care, ensuring he had the necessary medical insurance, the proper nutrition, and a living environment tailored to his health needs. Her life revolved around providing him with the best possible care.

However, while being so focused on her husband's health, the wife neglected her wellbeing. She overlooked the importance of regular health check-ups and self-care. Over time, this neglect led to her developing a serious health condition. Sadly, her illness progressed rapidly, leaving her unable to care for herself or her husband.

This situation is not uncommon in caregiving scenarios. Often, the primary caregiver in a family becomes so immersed in caring for their loved one that they forget to take care of their own health. This can lead to the caregiver's health deteriorating, sometimes even more rapidly than that of the person they are caring for.

In this case, by the time the wife sought help, it was too late. She passed away, leaving behind her husband, whom she had devotedly cared for. Her story is a stark reminder of the critical importance of self-care for caregivers. It highlights the reality that caregivers must prioritize their health to continue effectively providing care for their loved ones. Neglecting personal health can lead to severe consequences, not only for the caregiver but also for the person they are caring for.

Essential Self-Care Tip #1. Prioritize Your Physical Health

In an airplane cabin, a seemingly simple directive from the flight attendant carries profound wisdom that resonates far beyond the confines of the aircraft. As the voice calmly instructs passengers to secure their oxygen masks before assisting others in case of an emergency, it encapsulates a universal truth about the necessity of self-preservation as a precursor to effective caregiving.

This principle of prioritizing one's health is a cornerstone of responsible caregiving, echoing the axiom that one cannot pour from an empty cup. In the turbulence of living, just as in the unpredictability of flight, ensuring one's own well-being is not just an act of self-care but a strategic imperative to extend the best care to others.

Embracing this philosophy requires a commitment to regular health check-ups, which are recognized as essential touchpoints for preventative care and early detection of potential health concerns. These medical rendezvous serve as a barometer of your well-being, providing insights crucial to maintaining your health's equilibrium.

Another pillar of this approach is a balanced diet, rich in nutrients and tailored to your body's needs. It's about nurturing your body with the proper fuel and understanding that what you consume directly influences your capacity to thrive, endure, and care for others. It's not just about sustenance but about vitality and vigor.

Adequate rest, often underrated yet immensely powerful, is the silent regenerator of your physical strength and mental clarity. In the quietude of rest, your body repairs, your mind unwinds, and your spirit rejuvenates. In these moments of repose, you gather the strength to face new challenges and embrace the demands of caregiving with renewed energy and resilience.

This holistic approach to self-care, akin to the meticulous procedure of securing an oxygen mask, is not an indulgence but a fundamental duty. It's a testament to the understanding that the best way to extend care, compassion, and support to others is to ensure that you stand on a foundation of robust health and vitality.

Case Story #2

We often encounter deeply emotional and complex situations in our work with caregiving families. One particularly striking case involved a family seeking care for their mother with Dementia. The son, who had been her primary caregiver, was grappling with intense emotions and a sense of overwhelming responsibility. The role of the caregiver had taken a significant toll on his personal life, leading to feelings of resentment and frustration. These emotions, while difficult, are not uncommon in the caregiving landscape.

His struggle reached a boiling point where, in a moment of profound desperation and exhaustion, he confided in us with a startling admission: "I wish she would just fall down the stairs and break a hip so I could put her in a nursing home." This statement, though jarring, reflected the depth of his emotional turmoil. It illustrated the immense pressure caregivers often face, especially when they feel isolated in their responsibilities.

This expression of frustration and fatigue is a cry for help, a manifestation of the mental and emotional burden that comes with caring for a loved one with a debilitating condition. Family caregivers can find themselves performing tasks they never anticipated, such as managing incontinence or feeding a parent who may not recognize them anymore. This reversal of roles, from being cared for to being the caregiver, can be disorienting and painful.

The son's outburst underscored the importance of acknowledging and addressing caregivers' mental and emotional health. Caregivers must have access to support systems and self-care practices to navigate the complex emotions associated with caregiving. Feelings of resentment, anger, and grief are part of the process, and addressing them is key to maintaining the caregiver's well-being and ensuring they can continue to provide compassionate care.

In such situations, caregivers must recognize the need to take care of themselves, seek support, and understand that their feelings are valid. Caregiver burnout is a real and serious issue, and addressing it is vital for the health of both the caregiver and the person they are caring for.

Essential Self-Care Tip #2. Embrace Emotional Well-being

Embracing emotional well-being is essential, especially for caregivers who navigate high-stress and demanding emotional landscapes. Mental health, just as crucial as physical health, significantly influences our interactions and caregiving responsibilities. Integrating mindfulness, meditation, professional counseling, support groups, and self-compassion into daily life is beneficial and necessary for maintaining emotional balance and resilience.

Mindfulness & Meditation

This practice is far more than a contemporary trend; it's a transformative tool that anchors you in the present. Mindfulness helps alleviate the burden of past regrets and future worries by fully engaging in the now. Regular mindfulness practice can ease the mental load of caregiving, fostering a sense of calm and focus and making challenging situations more manageable. Meditation is a timeless practice that offers a quiet refuge to calm the mind and soul. Whether it's focusing on breathing, a word, or a phrase, meditation's benefits, such as lowering blood pressure and reducing anxiety, are well-documented. For caregivers, these benefits translate into better emotional control, enhanced patience, and a more profound sense of empathy.

Professional Counseling & Support Groups

Seeking professional help is a sign of strength, not weakness. Caregivers face unique challenges, from managing complex medical situations to handling emotional stress, which can be daunting. Counseling provides a safe space to express and process these feelings, offering vital coping strategies and support. Support groups provide invaluable support, allowing caregivers to connect with others in similar situations. Sharing experiences and advice in a supportive environment can be incredibly empowering, providing strength and comfort.

Self-Compassion

Self-compassion is a vital yet often neglected aspect of self-care, especially for those in caregiving roles. As caregivers, we are inherently attuned to the needs and well-being of others, sometimes to the point where our own needs are sidelined. However, it is crucial to understand that caring for oneself is not selfish but necessary to sustain our ability to care for others effectively. Treating oneself with kindness and understanding is the essence of self-compassion. It involves recognizing and appreciating the efforts we put into caregiving, even when they seem unnoticed or unappreciated by others. It's about acknowledging that, as caregivers, we are doing our best in challenging circumstances and that it's okay not to be perfect. Forgiving ourselves for mistakes is also a critical component of self-compassion. When acting as a caregiver, errors are inevitable. We must remember that mistakes do not define our worth or the value of our care. Instead, they are opportunities for learning and growth. Offering ourselves the same forgiveness and understanding that we would extend to others is vital in practicing self-compassion. Recognizing the necessity of self-love and self-care is equally important. This means allowing ourselves time and space to recharge, pursuing activities that bring us joy and relaxation, and setting boundaries to prevent burnout. It's about listening to our bodies and minds and allowing us to take breaks, seek support, and engage in activities that nurture our well-being. In essence, self-compassion is about treating ourselves with the same care and understanding we offer to those we care for. It's a reminder that our well-being is as important as those we care for. By embracing self-compassion, we enhance our lives and enrich the quality of care we provide to others.

Embracing the Love & Power of God

The directive in 1 Peter 5:7, "Cast all your anxiety on Him because He cares for you," reminds me that I am not alone in my struggles. There have been countless moments where the weight of caregiving responsibilities seemed insurmountable. This scripture has encouraged me to lay my burdens at His feet, trusting in God's unfailing care and support. It has taught me that in releasing my anxieties to Him, I find the strength to carry on, reassured by His presence and guidance. Philippians 4:6-16 has been a beacon of peace amidst the storm. "Do not be anxious about anything, but in everything by prayer and supplication with thanksgiving let your requests be made known to God. And the peace of God, which surpasses all understanding, will guard your hearts and your minds in Christ Jesus." In moments of uncertainty and worry, these verses have been a soothing balm, reminding me that I can turn to God in every situation in prayer. The peace that comes from this divine communion is beyond human comprehension, safeguarding my heart and mind and enabling me to navigate the complexities of caregiving with a serene spirit.

Practice and meditation have been vital elements of my life. They have provided a sacred space to communicate with God—to share my deepest fears, express my hopes, and offer my heartfelt gratitude. This communion has been a wellspring of clarity and peace, offering solace and direction when the path ahead seemed unclear. Being part of a supportive faith community has been incredibly uplifting. Sharing my story with others who understand and empathize with the challenges of caregiving has reinforced my resolve and faith.

This fellowship has been a source of collective strength and encouragement, reminding me that I am part of a larger body united in faith and purpose. Mindfulness in faith has enriched my daily walk with God. It has taught me to be present, to recognize His hand in the minutiae of life, and to listen attentively to His whispers of guidance and reassurance. This practice has brought a deeper appreciation for the beauty around me and a more profound awareness of God's constant presence. Jeremiah 29:11 has been a promise I hold close to my heart. "For I know the plans I have for you, declares the Lord, plans to prosper you and not to harm you, plans to give you hope and a future." In times of uncertainty and change, this scripture has reminded me of God's overarching plan for my life. It has given me the courage to trust in His path, even when it diverged from my plans, knowing that His intentions are always for my welfare and growth. These spiritual truths have been instrumental in shaping my approach to caregiving and life. They have provided comfort, strength, and guidance, reinforcing that while I care for others, I am also lovingly held and guided by a higher power.

Case Study #3

In our experience with caregiving, we often encounter situations where the boundaries between helping and enabling become blurred. One such case involved a woman who reached out to us for assistance with her neighbor. She had known this neighbor for many years and had witnessed her struggle to maintain independence in her home. As the neighbor aged and her health deteriorated, the situation became increasingly concerning. The neighbor, who was wheelchair-bound and without family support, had developed a hoarding problem. Her house was cluttered with debris, old food, and other refuse. Compounding the issue, she had several pets whose needs were not adequately met, leading to unsanitary conditions within the home. Despite these challenges, the neighbor was adamant about not letting anyone into her house except for the woman who contacted us.

The concerned neighbor described feeling caught in a difficult position. She would visit to sit, chat, and occasionally help with meals, but each visit made her increasingly aware of her neighbor's dire living conditions. Her presence, she feared, was inadvertently enabling her neighbor's refusal to seek professional help. The more she assisted, the less incentive her neighbor had to accept the care she truly needed. Faced with this dilemma, the woman realized the importance of setting boundaries. She understood that her well-intentioned visits while offering temporary relief, were not addressing the underlying issues. Her neighbor needed professional care and a safer living environment, which she could not provide alone.

This realization led to a critical decision. She approached us, seeking guidance on how to best support her neighbor by getting the professional help she needed. This step was about more than just distancing herself; it was about ensuring her neighbor received appropriate care in a safe, healthy environment.

The situation highlighted the delicate balance caregivers must navigate—providing support without enabling detrimental behaviors. It underscored the importance of recognizing when professional intervention is necessary and taking steps to facilitate it, even when it means stepping back. In doing so, caregivers can help their loved ones receive the comprehensive care they need while also preserving their own well-being.

Essential Self-Care Tip #3. Set Boundaries

Setting boundaries is an essential yet challenging aspect of being a family caregiver. The role often blurs the lines between duty, love, and self-sacrifice, making it difficult to establish personal limits. However, recognizing the importance of saying 'no' and maintaining boundaries is crucial for preserving one's health, relationships, and the overall quality of care.

Without boundaries, caregivers can quickly become overextended, leading to burnout. This state of physical, emotional, and mental exhaustion not only harms the caregiver's health but also affects their ability to provide adequate care. Furthermore, continuously prioritizing others' needs without setting limits can lead to feelings of resentment. Such emotions can strain friendships and family relationships, creating a tense and unhealthy caregiving environment. Moreover, neglecting personal health needs due to a lack of boundaries can lead to a decline in the caregiver's physical and mental health.

This impacts the caregiver and the person they are caring for. Additionally, caregivers who do not set boundaries may lose their sense of self. They might neglect their hobbies, interests, and social connections, leading to a loss of personal identity and fulfillment.

Caregivers should begin by understanding their physical, emotional, and mental limits to effectively set boundaries. It's crucial to recognize the signs that indicate they're reaching these limits, such as feelings of exhaustion, irritability, or anxiety. Communicating these needs and limits to family members clearly and assertively is critical, and it should be done respectfully and straightforwardly.

Learning to say 'no' to requests that are beyond one's capacity is a critical practice. It's vital to remember that saying 'no' is not a sign of failure or lack of compassion but a necessary step to maintain well-being and the quality of care provided.

In summary, setting boundaries in caregiving is not about shirking responsibilities but about maintaining a sustainable balance that benefits both the caregiver and the care recipient. It's a vital aspect of caregiving that ensures the caregiver's health and well-being, thereby enabling them to provide the best possible care over the long term.

Case Study #4

Amid her caregiving responsibilities, one of our clients found herself navigating a delicate balance between her devotion to her husband and her own personal needs. As a naturally sociable person, her life was previously filled with the joys of bridge games, sewing classes, and the warm companionship of her friends. These activities were more than hobbies; they were her connection to a world outside the confines of her caregiving duties, a world that brought her laughter, a sense of community, and happiness.

Her husband, needing her care and company, became the center of her world. While our team assisted during the day, her evenings were reserved exclusively for him. Gradually, the life she once knew, filled with social gatherings and shared moments with friends, faded into the background. She confided in us her longing to return to those joyful evenings, to engage in lively board games, to share stories of their lives, and to reminisce with her friends. She missed exchanging photos of their grandchildren and witnessing the passage of time through their growth.

Her love for her husband was profound and unwavering, yet she couldn't help but feel a sense of loss for herself. She was torn between the guilt of wanting to engage in activities she loved and the desire to always be there for her husband. This internal conflict created a sense of solitude, as she felt increasingly isolated in her home. This situation shows a critical truth about caregiving: the importance of maintaining one's own identity and emotional health. For our client, reconnecting with her passions and friendships was not just a desire but a necessity for her well-being. The fulfillment derived from personal interests and social interactions is crucial for caregivers to maintain their sense of self.

Her story is a poignant reminder of the essential balance that caregivers must strike. Caregivers must allow themselves the space and time to indulge in personal interests and maintain social connections. This is not an act of selfishness but a recognition that to care effectively for others; one must also take care of oneself. It's a balance of nurturing the spirit and fulfilling responsibilities, ensuring that one does not lose themselves in the process of caregiving.

Essential Self-Care Tip #4. Engage in Self-reflection & Personal Rejuvenation Activities

Regularly reflect on your feelings and experiences. This helps you understand your limits and recognize when you need a break. Engaging in personal rejuvenation activities beyond caregiving is also essential. Whether pursuing a hobby, enjoying social outings, or simply taking time to be still and reflect, these activities contribute significantly to a caregiver's well-being. They provide a much-needed diversion from caregiving's demands, helping maintain a sense of individuality and personal fulfillment.

Scheduled Self-Reflection Time

Dedicate a specific time each day or week for self-reflection. This could be early morning, before the rest of the household wakes up, or late at night when things have settled down. The key is to find a quiet time that works for you.

Journaling

Keep a journal to document your thoughts, feelings, and experiences. Writing down your reflections can provide clarity, help process emotions, and track changes over time. It can be as simple as noting down a few thoughts or as detailed as describing the day's events and your reactions to them.

Pursuing a Hobby

Identify and dedicate time to a hobby or interest that brings you joy. Hobbies can be anything from gardening to painting to playing a musical instrument to crafting. They provide a creative outlet and a break from the routine of caregiving.

Social Outings

Plan outings with friends or attend social gatherings regularly. These could include coffee dates, movie nights, or community events. Social interactions are crucial for mental health and provide a sense of normalcy and connection to the world outside of caregiving.

Quiet Contemplation

Allocate time for quiet contemplation or relaxation. This could involve reading a book, listening to music, or simply sitting in a peaceful spot. These moments of stillness can be profoundly rejuvenating, allowing you to disconnect from the demands of caregiving and reconnect with yourself.

Nature Walks

Spend time in nature, whether walking in the park, hiking in the woods, or just sitting in a garden. Being in natural surroundings can be incredibly therapeutic, offering a calm and fresh perspective.

By incorporating these practices into your routine, you create a balanced approach to caregiving. Regular self-reflection helps you understand your emotional and physical limits, signaling when to take a break. Engaging in personal rejuvenation activities ensures that you maintain your sense of self, contributing to your overall happiness and effectiveness as a caregiver. These practices are beneficial for your well-being and essential in sustaining the energy and compassion required for caregiving.

Case study #5

In a story that resonates with many families, we encountered a situation that exemplifies the power and necessity of a robust support system. This story begins with a family whose life was upended by their daughter's sudden illness. The parents, deeply committed to their daughter's well-being, found themselves entrenched in a relentless routine of doctor's appointments and hospital stays, tirelessly striving to provide the care she needed.

Amidst this turmoil, the couple faced the challenging reality that their two other teenage children also needed attention and care. Their family life had become a juggling act of hospital visits and managing the day-to-day needs of their household, leaving little room for anything else. The strain of their daughter's illness began to seep into every aspect of their lives, including their marriage. The simple joys of date nights and quality time together had fallen by the wayside, eclipsed by the enormity of their caregiving responsibilities.

Recognizing the unsustainable nature of their situation, the couple turned to their church community for support. They proactively requested help through a meal chain to ease the burden of meal preparation for their family. They sought assistance with clothing for their daughter and outings for their other children, aiming to bring a sense of normalcy back into their lives. Their request for help extended further, asking their church friends and family to sit with their daughter at the hospital occasionally. This small act of kindness granted them precious moments to reconnect as a couple, preserving the strength of their marriage amidst the trials they faced.

Their community responded with overwhelming support. Friends and church members stepped in, providing meals, assistance around the house, and much-needed companionship for their daughter during hospital stays. Their daughter's illness had not only transformed their lives but also laid bare the pressing need for a reliable, compassionate support system. Amid the whirlwind of hospital visits, caring for their other children, and striving to maintain a normal family life, they realized that the support they required was beyond the scope of occasional assistance.

It was then that they turned to the best caregiving company they knew—one that epitomized compassion and professionalism. Remarkably, this was not just any caregiving service. It was I-CARE Home Health Care, the very company they had founded. This story, incredibly, is about my husband and me. We found ourselves in desperate need of the services we had created to aid others, a testament to life's unpredictable turns.

We founded I-CARE Home Health Care in 1993, a whole 11 years before our daughter Ashley was diagnosed with Multiple Sclerosis. Little did we know then that the service we had started to help others would become our lifeline. In our hour of greatest need, we relied on I-CARE, trusting in the exceptional care and support it was known for, to help our family navigate this challenging period.

This experience not only emphasizes the importance of cultivating a robust support system but also highlights the unpredictable nature of life. It reinforced the belief that sometimes, the help we extend to others can circle back to support us in our times of need. We continue to be immensely grateful that God blessed us with I-CARE, a resource that not only served our community but became a crucial part of our family. This story is a poignant reminder of how life can come full circle and how the seeds we plant in service to others can grow to sustain us in our times of need. In addition, our family's experience highlights the importance of cultivating a robust support system. It demonstrates how reaching out for help, building a community of support, and seeking professional care can be pivotal in navigating the complexities of caregiving. Our story is a testament to the strength found in the community, the resilience of families, and the profound impact of compassionate care.

Essential Self-Care Tip #5. Cultivate a Support System

Surround yourself with people who understand, support, and uplift you. Having a network to lean on can significantly reduce the burden of caregiving. Caregivers should not hesitate to ask for help. Engaging other family members, friends, or professional caregivers can provide respite and ensure that the care recipient's needs are met. It is also crucial to prioritize self-care activities that rejuvenate, whether it's a hobby, exercise, socializing, or simply resting.

Creating a robust support network is a critical element in a caregiver's life, providing both emotional and practical assistance. Surrounding themselves with understanding and supportive individuals, including family, friends, and professional services, can significantly alleviate the caregiving burden.

Family and friends play a vital role in this network. They can step in to share caregiving duties, offering the primary caregiver essential breaks for personal time. This respite is an opportunity to engage in cherished hobbies or activities set aside due to caregiving responsibilities. It's a chance to reconnect with oneself and rejuvenate.

Professional caregiver services are often invaluable to a caregiver's support system. Recognizing the need for professional and compassionate caregiving support, I founded I-CARE Inc. to assist families in these exact situations. Whether providing a few hours of care daily or offering total live-in assistance, I-CARE Inc. is dedicated to helping families manage their caregiving needs, especially for those who may live far away from their loved ones. Our team of qualified professionals ensures that families receive the help they need, bringing peace of mind to the caregivers and those they care for.

In addition to family, friends, and professional help, having a church family can be a tremendous source of support. In times of difficulty or exhaustion, a church community can offer much-needed encouragement and practical assistance. They can be a shoulder to lean on, offering spiritual guidance and tangible help in times of need. The sense of belonging and collective strength within a church family can be a wellspring of comfort and hope for caregivers.

Together, this multifaceted support network plays a pivotal role in the life of a caregiver. It helps ease caregiving's physical and emotional strains, ensuring that caregivers have the necessary resources and support. This network enables caregivers to continue their essential work with resilience, strength, and compassion, making a significant difference in the lives of those they care for.

These five principles transformed into my shield and source of strength as I navigated the realms of healthcare and advocacy. They transitioned from mere concepts to tangible experiences, each highlighting the critical role of self-care in the caregiving journey.

Chapter 2

Early Aspirations to Advocacy
Donna's Youthful Dive into Healthcare

In this chapter, I share a critical phase of my life, blending my academic pursuits with the challenges of navigating personal health issues and the initial steps into the healthcare arena. It captures a period of growth and discovery, from the excitement of exploring potential careers to the realities of confronting health obstacles and venturing into the professional world. This quest, marked by leadership roles and a commitment to making a difference, sets the stage for my advocacy in healthcare. It reflects on overcoming adversity, learning from early experiences, and the determination to contribute meaningfully to the field. As I recount these formative years, I also offer valuable insights gained along the way—lessons in resilience, adaptability, and the importance of nurturing one's passion. These insights, born from my youthful academic and personal endeavors, are shared as tips for young individuals to guide them through their journeys toward impactful and fulfilling careers in healthcare.

From Curiosity to Career: My STEM Journey Begins

At the young age of 14, nestled within the vibrant yet challenging landscapes of Toledo, Ohio, my future as a stalwart advocate for healthcare began. This chapter of my life unfolded within the bounds of the Explorers program, a beacon for high school students intrigued by the vast and ever-evolving realm of medical careers. As I assumed the mantle of leadership, overseeing a contingent of 200 peers, we stood at the threshold of a new era, one ripe with the promise of medical advancements and technological breakthroughs. The year was 1977, and we were on the cusp of witnessing revolutionary developments in the field of medicine:

The first MRI Exam was performed on a human being, opening a new window into the human body without invasive surgery. The introduction of the CT (Computed Tomography) scanner revolutionized detailed brain imaging, allowing for unprecedented clarity and precision.

By 1978, the approval of the first recombinant DNA drug, human insulin, by Genentech, heralded the era of biotechnology in medicine, transforming the treatment of diabetes. Advancements in laparoscopic surgery techniques were leading the way towards less invasive surgical procedures, significantly reducing recovery times and risks associated with open surgeries. The emergence of PET (Positron Emission Tomography) scanning technology began to offer new insights into metabolic processes in the body, paving the way for more accurate diagnoses and personalized medicine.

These advancements captured my imagination and solidified my resolve to be at the forefront of healthcare and innovation. As we delved into the intricacies of science and medicine, I was mesmerized by the potential of these technologies to transform patient care. It was a formative period that underscored my commitment to pursuing a career that blended my passion for science with a deep-seated desire to advocate for patient well-being and advance healthcare excellence. My experiences during this pivotal time laid the groundwork for my future endeavors, inspiring me to chart new waters from academic pursuits to healthcare advocacy.

The program's curriculum was both daunting and exhilarating, offering hands-on experiences. Among these was the dissection of a frog, an exercise that, despite its initial grimness, unveiled the wonders of biological science. The complexity and harmony of the frog's anatomy were a revelation, showcasing the interconnectedness of life's systems. Leadership within the Explorers program transcended the conventional; it allowed me to mold futures and illuminate paths for my peers. The position was a conduit through which I could channel my enthusiasm for science and medicine, guiding others toward fulfilling careers in healthcare. The experience was pivotal, not only for those I led but for myself as well, as it highlighted the significant influence of leadership in shaping individuals' aspirations and careers.

This continued as I ventured into higher education at the age of 15, courtesy of a grant that allowed me to immerse myself in the world of chemistry labs over the summer. This foray into academic science was enthralling, presenting a universe where liquids and chemicals conversed in the language of reactions, where every experiment was a step toward unraveling the mysteries of the natural world. My engagement with chemistry was more than academic curiosity; it was a pursuit laden with purpose and the promise of making a tangible difference in the world.

Inspired by these experiences and an insatiable eagerness to delve deeper into the sciences, I decided to accelerate my high school education. This resolve saw me graduating high school a year early. My path led me to Bowling Green State University (BGSU) in Ohio, where, at 16, I embarked on a major in Chemistry Pre-Med. This decision was not merely academic; it was a declaration of my commitment to healthcare and leadership. The Explorers program laid the foundation, revealing to me the unparalleled impact that informed, compassionate leadership could have in the medical field.

During my academic tenure in the Chemistry Pre-Med program, my ambitions became clear and defined. I saw myself evolving, not merely into a physician but as a guiding force and advocate, leveraging scientific knowledge and compassion to create avenues for improved health outcomes. This study period was marked by a growing realization of my potential to impact the healthcare landscape far beyond the laboratory or lecture hall. It was a foundational phase, shaping me into an advocate ready to navigate and demystify the complexities of healthcare for others. My experience in this field transformed me into a leader poised to contribute to a more knowledgeable and healthier community. This was not just about acquiring a degree; it was about preparing to make a meaningful difference in the lives of individuals navigating their health pilgrimage, armed with the conviction that informed advocacy could lead to transformative health outcomes.

Empowering Your Path in Healthcare
Five Essential Insights for Aspiring Medical Professionals

1. Embrace Curiosity and Innovation

My early fascination with groundbreaking medical technologies, from MRI exams to the first recombinant DNA drugs, taught me the importance of curiosity and innovation in healthcare. For young adults entering the medical field, staying abreast of the latest advancements and thinking innovatively can transform patient care. Always seek to learn and embrace the rapid evolution of medical science as a constant in your career.

2. Pursue Hands-on Experience

Just as dissecting a frog opened my eyes to the wonders of biology, hands-on experiences are invaluable. Whether through internships, volunteer work, or lab research, real-world experience provides a deeper understanding of medical science and patient care. Seek opportunities to apply your knowledge practically, as these experiences enrich your learning and make you a more compassionate caregiver.

3. Cultivate Leadership Skills

Over 200 peers in the Explorers program have emphasized the importance of effective leadership in healthcare. As you begin your career, it is crucial to develop your leadership abilities. This may involve taking the lead in group projects, mentoring others, or participating in community service. Having strong leadership skills will help you advocate more effectively for your patients and lead teams toward innovative solutions.

4. Accelerate Your Education When Possible

My decision to graduate high school early and major in Chemistry Pre-Med was driven by a desire to quickly engage with my passion. If you're driven and ready, consider pathways that accelerate your entry into healthcare. Advanced placement courses, dual enrollment, and summer academic programs can provide a head start in your medical education.

5. Commit to Lifelong Learning and Advocacy

The transition from academic pursuits to healthcare advocacy wasn't just about acquiring a degree but about preparing to make a meaningful difference. In healthcare, your education never truly ends. Commit to lifelong learning to enhance your skills and become a better advocate for your patients. Embrace the role of advocate, using your knowledge and voice to improve the healthcare system and patient outcomes.

These tips, drawn from my experiences, are designed to guide young adults through their foray into the medical field. They emphasize the importance of curiosity, hands-on experience, leadership, educational acceleration, and a commitment to lifelong learning and advocacy. Each is a cornerstone for building a fulfilling and impactful career in healthcare.

Navigating Life's Detours: Embracing Change and Perseverance

After spending a year at Bowling Green State University, my life took an unexpected detour. My mother's career led our family from the familiar grounds of Ohio to the uncharted territory of Oklahoma, presenting a new chapter filled with opportunities and challenges. This move wasn't merely a change of scenery but a shift in my personal and academic goals.

At Oklahoma State University, I found myself in a vibrant new academic environment, yet it was outside the classroom that a significant chapter of my life began to unfold. In January of 1982, amidst the challenges of adjusting to a new state and university, I crossed paths with Anthony Ivey. Our meeting wasn't planned, but the connection was instantaneous and profound. With his charismatic smile and genuine kindness, Anthony brought a sense of stability and hope during a time of significant change. His devout Christian faith and compassionate worldview resonated deeply with me, offering a sense of belonging and partnership I hadn't realized I was seeking.

The initial excitement of our relationship soon faced the realities of life's unpredictability. My health challenges, marked by frequent hospitalizations, emerged as a recurring theme that not only tested the resilience of our new relationship but also presented significant hurdles to my academic pursuits and aspirations within the healthcare field. My academic ambitions at Oklahoma State University were put on hold with my mother embarking on her trip to Mexico and my financial support waning. The decision to leave university in 1985 was difficult, yet it marked the beginning of a new chapter that would eventually lead to the birth of our daughter, Ashley, and the deepening of my resolve to pursue a career in healthcare.

During pregnancy, I also found a confidante and mentor in my Aunt Lavell. Mentoring is very important at any age, especially as you battle the unknown. Motherhood was an unknown, and because my mom was in Mexico, I knew I needed someone to help me navigate my new life. Having walked a similar road herself, Aunt Lavell had objective guidance and insight. She used her experiences to embrace the positive and shared her gifts and resources to help others. She opened her home to others and showed generosity and unconditional love. I watched her and am inspired to channel her example in my life. My Aunt's mothering mentorship and spiritual guidance encouraged me to foster my spiritual growth and development.

In Ohio, when I was pregnant, I found a job at a hospital daycare center making $3.35 an hour. I had no transportation then, received government services, and had no permanent home. I was essentially homeless and bounced around from my relative's home to my relative's house.

When Ashley was born, the daycare center where I worked allowed me to bring her to work for free. Bringing Ashley to work with me was a blessing; it allowed me to care for her while gaining insights from observing the family dynamics of doctors and nurses. Over nearly two years as I worked there, I was enveloped in the daily lives of these children, seeing firsthand how they mirrored their parents' behaviors and personalities. For instance, children of surgeons often showed a remarkable ability to focus intently on tasks, just as their parents would during surgery. Meanwhile, the children of pediatricians displayed a natural ease and comfort around others, reflecting the compassionate nature of their parents' work. This experience shaped how I raised my children and strengthened my dedication to advocating for a comprehensive approach to healthcare that emphasizes the family's vital contribution to a patient's health and happiness. Although I wasn't directly working in healthcare at the time, I felt a strong connection to the children and their parents. Caring for these children during the day while their parents were busy working at the hospital was an honor. I felt like I was contributing to the healthcare system by providing peace of mind to the parents working there. Knowing their children were in good hands with me allowed them to focus on their jobs and help others.

Anthony graduated from Oklahoma State University in 1986 and moved in March of 1987 to Virginia to become a Construction Field Inspector for the Virginia Department of Transportation. He worked diligently in Virginia to prepare a better life for us and Ashley. I arrived in Virginia in 1987 with three things: an 18-month-old Ashley, a duffle bag, and a footlocker. It was our new beginning, and we were eager to lay down roots and contribute to our new community. Together, with the support of Tony's sister, who allowed us to move in, we began our new life in Northern Virginia. As my husband Anthony and I began our new life together in Northern Virginia, my career took a significant turn that would shape my perspective on healthcare forever. During this period, filled with the challenges of adapting to a new environment, balancing work, and starting a family, I found myself working at a neurologist's office as an administrative assistant. This experience would deepen my commitment to making a meaningful difference in healthcare and illuminate the complexities faced by those navigating neurological conditions.

Five Guiding Principles for Navigating Life's Changes

Life throws challenges at us at every stage, and throughout moving, facing health issues, and career shifts, I've learned valuable lessons applicable to both young and older adults. These lessons have emerged as guiding principles for navigating the unpredictable waters of life. Here are five crucial tips, each born from personal experiences, that I've found particularly helpful for individuals across different ages. They offer insight into adapting to change, the importance of supportive relationships, the power of resilience, the value of mentorship, and the significance of holding onto your dreams. Whether you're just starting or looking back on a life full of stories, these tips can provide direction and encouragement as you navigate your path.

1. Embrace Change with Open Arms

My move from Ohio to Oklahoma highlighted life's unpredictability, which I initially found daunting. Yet, embracing change as a catalyst for growth has been enriching. Each shift, whether chosen or unforeseen, presents a chance to learn and evolve. Like navigating a new city, adapting to change can uncover paths and opportunities that enrich our lives, reminding us that growth often requires stepping out of our comfort zones.

2. Find Strength in Relationships

During my transition, the stability provided by my relationship with Anthony was invaluable. Surrounding yourself with supportive individuals, those who understand and encourage your aspirations is crucial. Much like a lighthouse in a storm, these relationships offer guidance and comfort, illuminating our way through the darkest times and celebrating our victories, big and small.

3. Persevere Through Challenges

My encounters with health issues and academic obstacles underscored the essence of resilience. The steadfast pursuit of our goals, despite the hurdles, carves our path. This resilience, a testament to our inner strength, teaches us that our reaction to adversity ultimately shapes our destiny and defines our successes.

4. Seek Guidance and Mentorship

Just as Aunt Lavell has been a guiding force, mentors serve as a navigational aid through the uncertainties of life. They share wisdom from their own experiences, lend a sympathetic ear to our concerns, and offer comfort during times of hesitation. By connecting with individuals who have faced similar challenges, we can gain insights that clear the way forward, enhancing our resolve and assurance as we continue our journey.

5. Hold onto Your Dreams

My life's path, from aspiring to work in healthcare to finding a fulfilling role in a hospital daycare before settling in Virginia, taught me the enduring nature of dreams. They persist beyond detours and delays, urging us to press on. Our dreams may require patience, flexibility, and tenacity, but holding fast to them, even when the route diverges from our planned course, can lead to achievements beyond our original imaginings. Dreams remind us that with persistence, the possibilities are limitless.

Health Care Administrative Experience
Where I Learned the Importance of Having an Advocate

In the dynamic setting of a neurologist's office that housed five of the region's most renowned and sought-after neurologists, my position took on dimensions that far surpassed typical administrative duties. This wasn't just any neurologist's office; it was a place where patients came hoping to find answers and relief from their neurological symptoms and conditions. The renowned status of our neurologists meant that our office was constantly busy, a testament to the trust and reputation they had built in the field. Our administrative assistants played a crucial role in managing this flow of activity, ensuring that each patient received the attention and care they sought. Alongside five other administrative assistants, we formed the front line of the practice, fielding calls, welcoming patients, and meticulously preparing charts for the doctors.

Every day brought new challenges and learning opportunities as I navigated the complexities of scheduling, patient communication, and chart preparation. The experience was profoundly educational, offering me a unique vantage point into the intricacies of neurological care and the profound impact of diseases like ALS, Parkinson's, and Multiple Sclerosis on individuals and their families. I gained invaluable insights into the emotional and physical struggles of those affected by neurological conditions. It was a privilege to be part of a team that contributed to their care, even in the seemingly small yet significant ways of ensuring the smooth operation of the office. This period of my career was not just about fulfilling administrative tasks; it was about being part of a collective effort to provide hope and support to those navigating the complexities of neurological diseases.

Patients who came to our office sought not just medical treatment but understanding, support, and a welcoming smile. Observing these patients, some of whom navigated the office corridors unaided while others leaned on the support of wheelchairs or walkers, I was struck by the diversity of their abilities and experiences. It was a profoundly educational period for me, bridging the gap between the clinical descriptions of diseases I had read about in charts and the real-life implications of those conditions. Patients came in all states of their illness—some newly diagnosed, trying to wrap their heads around the uncertainty of their future, and others well into their battle with the disease, displaying an array of emotions from determination to despair.

At the office, I encountered patients with strong support networks and others braving their conditions solo, highlighting the critical importance of community and advocacy in healthcare. The individuals who did not have a support system or advocate had to understand medical advice and directives from the neurologists, handle their insurance and the finances of their medical care, and deal with their illness entirely on their own. In contrast, patients with supportive advocacy networks fared better, benefiting from assistance in managing their condition and the financial implications of the illness. The financial strain of managing a chronic illness was a familiar story to me, echoing my own family's experiences with healthcare challenges. These observations showed that support and advocacy significantly influence patient care outcomes. It reinforced my determination to be as effective an advocate as possible for my patients, understanding that help can dramatically improve the care and support they receive.

Working at a neurologist's office was more than just a job; it was an immersive learning experience that brought me face-to-face with the realities of neurological diseases. Working alongside neurologists, I saw reflections of my struggles in the patients we served. My experiences with recurring health challenges and hospitalizations, starting from childhood and extending through college, had already given me a firsthand understanding of how health issues can profoundly affect one's life.

Witnessing the varied responses to these diseases, from those grappling with fear and concern to uncovering hope amidst the most demanding challenges, was eye-opening. It reinforced the importance of empathy and the need for a healthcare system that addresses physical health and the emotional and mental well-being of patients and their families. Though administrative, my role in the office was part of a more significant effort in patient care. From neurologists making life-changing diagnoses to administrative staff like myself, ensuring the smooth operation of the practice, we each played a part in the broader mission of patient care. It was a powerful reminder that no contribution is too small in healthcare, and every effort toward supporting patients' health and well-being is valuable.

While at a neurology office, I embarked on a transformative journey that significantly shaped my career in healthcare advocacy and profoundly impacted my personal life. Seeing patients face their challenges with resilience and courage every day inspired me to dedicate myself to simplifying the complexities they encountered within the healthcare system. This role enhanced my patient care and advocacy skills, highlighting the essential need for a healthcare system that truly meets patient needs.

My interest in becoming a healthcare advocate was influenced by my academic background in Chemistry Pre-Med and enriched by practical experiences that bridged theory with real-world application. This path revealed a career that could harmonize my passions for science, leadership, and service. Encountering personal and caregiving challenges reinforced my dedication to advocating for patient care and healthcare excellence. The strength and hope I admired in patients soon became my own, preparing me for future challenges, particularly in caring for my daughter, Ashley.

Working in the neurologist's office went beyond a regular job; it was an in-depth lesson in empathy, human health complexity, and the balance between medical science and individual resilience. This experience laid the foundation for my future in healthcare advocacy, especially in supporting Ashley. I directly observed the positive impact of having support and advocacy on patients, noting significantly better health outcomes for those with robust support systems. This realization propelled me toward advocating for a compassionate, supportive healthcare system that recognizes the importance of advocacy in patient care.

This chapter in my career was not just a step toward professional growth but a leap into a lifelong commitment to making a meaningful difference in the healthcare field. It confirmed my belief in the power of compassionate care and the crucial role of advocacy in improving patient outcomes, setting the stage for my continued efforts to champion healthcare excellence and patient-centered care.

Chapter 3

God's Strategic Plan Continues to Unfold
Entrepreneurship, Family, and Faith

God meticulously arranged support systems in my life long before I realized their significance. Owning my business was not just a career choice; it was a divine set-up that allowed me the freedom to be there for my daughter during her hospital visits, ensuring I could be present when it mattered most. Remarkably, my venture into the healthcare sector provided me with invaluable connections and an understanding of medical terminology, equipping me to secure the best possible care for my daughter.

By having all my children work in the company from 14, I unknowingly prepared a safety net for Ashley. This employment instilled in them a strong work ethic and integrated Ashley into the Medicare system as a W2 employee. This foresight meant she was fully covered by insurance when her health challenges arose, a blessing we could not have anticipated.

Moreover, the nurturing church family we cultivated over the years became a pillar of strength and support for Ashley and our entire family. Their presence and prayers carried us through the most challenging times, underscoring the importance of community in facing life's trials.

God's strategic plan placed all these pieces into alignment before I could even grasp the depth of our need. This divine orchestration allowed me to transition seamlessly into the dual roles of a family caregiver and a staunch advocate for my daughter, backed by a robust support system that was God-sent. In the following narrative, I will explore the genesis of my entrepreneurial venture, my children's integral role in our family business, and the profound impact of our spiritual life on navigating the challenges of Ashley's illness.

The Miracle of a Closed Door

In 1990, the job at the neurologist's office promoted me to work on a business project of theirs. They set me up at home and allowed me to work from there. I was very excited because, by this time, I had three children, my youngest being one month old. My career was looking up, and I was steadily getting more and more into health care. But as things happened, they changed very quickly. The job I loved so much decided to close the new venture and asked me to return to the office to work administratively. I had three children under four years old and couldn't return to work. My husband also lost his job around the same time. We were at a crucial time in our lives, homeowners with three young children, and we were both jobless.

Just before our layoffs, Tony and I had worked hard to get ourselves out of debt. We participated in a church program encouraging financial responsibility among Christians and subsequently celebrated becoming debt-free by cutting our credit cards. But, now what? We were both concerned about how we would make it and whether I needed to work as a CPR instructor or go back to complete school until Tony found a new position. We had three children, no work, and no credit cards. However, I knew that when God closes one door, He opens another.

I had the passion and drive to do something innovative, but it would take a lot of work and sacrifice. We ordered another Montgomery Ward credit card, and I bought my first Compaq computer with that card. It was with this computer that I began the business aspect of I-CARE. I had no prior business experience, and my goals needed fine-tuning, but I was committed to using my healthcare knowledge and training to help advocate and care for patients. To legally establish the company, I went to the library and looked up any similar names using Microfilm and Microfiche. Now, you can do this online!

In 1994, Tony took a year off from Construction Management to help me write the regulations for a home care organization and manage our rehab staff. He then returned to the construction industry for eight years until I-CARE grew to the point of being able to support our entire family. Therefore, he returned to I-CARE full-time in 2002. This was truly an "all our eggs were in one basket":" which was a faith walk to believe back then, that I-CARE.

The genesis of I-CARE was a testament to the power of vision, perseverance, and the belief that with hard work and faith, dreams can be turned into reality. It was a sojourn marked by challenges, learning, and growth, but above all, it was fueled by a desire to make a difference in the lives of those we serve.

To help restore excellence in healthcare, I felt I needed to further my education in business to make sure the infrastructure of healthcare was sustained by not only my life experience, but also more education in business practices and strategies. In 1997, after I began I-CARE. I continued my bachelor's degree, shifting my young adult focus from chemistry pre-med to business administration. My mother-in-law, Rosia Lee, was an instrumental encouragement and mentor to continue my education despite the new demands on my time with my family and business. She often asked during our phone calls, "Donna, now are you returning to school? You're like another daughter to me." The way she cared for me and asked was so endearing that I wanted to answer her questions with a yes. It was a long road, and I took one step at a time, shifting my courses as my personal or business demands changed. But after seven years, I graduated cum laude in 2003 and supplemented what I was learning on the ground at I-CARE with academic strategies to improve and expand our business.

I-CARE, symbolizing my commitment to "I Care About Restoring Excellence in Healthcare," became a tangible manifestation of my dream to provide compassionate, comprehensive care to those in need. From its inception, I-CARE was envisioned as a service grounded in excellence, empathy, and unwavering support for our clients and their families. I-CARE® Inc. stands for I Care About Restoring Excellence in Health Care. I-CARE, what I like to call my fourth baby, is a business we began with care at the core. Our team works with families in Northern Virginia to provide all aspects of nursing and personal care for clients of all ages who are homebound with illness, recovering from injury, or need assistance to remain safe at home. Our team partners with families utilizing experienced and involved nurses and caregivers who provide compassionate, detailed care to our patients. We educate patients on their condition and treatment options and use our healthcare system knowledge to offer their families guidance and support. We work to ensure our patients have their wishes respected and needs met. The company of I-CARE continues the thread of my desire to help others in their time of need. I-CARE has allowed me to be on the ground in people's homes and involved in their lives. For our first 10 years, I-CARE® Inc. focused on rehabilitation staffing for personal injuries and illnesses. I had experience in rehabilitation therapy, so I was comfortable with this plan. But in 2004, our business focus changed as our personal lives did. Tony and I personally saw gaps that needed addressing in healthcare.

Family Incorporation into the Business

Incorporating family into I-CARE went hand in hand with being a mother, where nurturing my children's growth extended well beyond traditional schooling. I endeavored to turn every moment into a learning opportunity. For instance, summers at our house blended physical play and intellectual stimulation. If the kids wanted to watch TV, they had to write a detailed summary of the episode, honing their writing and critical thinking skills, regardless of whether it was educational content or entertainment. This practice nurtured a love for writing and an appreciation for articulate expression.

Starting at a young age, I learned to find areas to educate my children beyond traditional schooling. Some involved creating classrooms in our home and timed activities on their summer school breaks to keep them active and engaged in learning. I would take Ashley to the teacher's store, and she would pick out learning assignments and games to teach her younger siblings. To instill the value of proper communication, I'd gently fine them for grammatical slips, turning it into a game where they'd scramble to find coins for their 'grammar jar.' This improved their speech and made them more mindful of how they expressed themselves.

My approach to integrating them into I-CARE at 14 was deliberate. Beyond giving them a worker's permit and a celebratory cake, it was about teaching them the real-world workings of employment and responsibility. They weren't just my children within the company; they were employees expected to meet the same standards as anyone else—punctuality, professionalism, and positivity. This experience was invaluable, particularly for Ashley, whose employment from a young age played a crucial role in her healthcare coverage when she faced her health challenges at 18.

Ashley, April, and Anthony Jr. learned the ins and outs of a professional environment early on, even participating in the interviewing processes. Observing and taking notes during interviews, they gained insights into what makes a candidate stand out: preparation, knowledge, and skill. This wasn't just about giving them a job; it was about preparing them for the world, ensuring they understood the value of hard work and the nuances of being part of a workforce.

This blend of home education and early professional experience paid dividends. It prepared them academically, earning them merit scholarships and prestigious college admissions, and equipped them with a work ethic and professional savvy that many their age lacked. By their mid-twenties, they had a decade of work experience under their belts, setting them apart in their respective fields.

My parenting and business integration strategy was guided by a belief that I was doing what was best for my children and our family. Guided by this conviction, I aimed to instill in them the importance of hard work, integrity, and a commitment to excellence. This approach has shaped our family's future toward success and fulfillment and has become a foundational principle of I-CARE.

Chapter 4

Navigating the Storm
The Dual Role of Family Caregiver and Advocate

Caring for a loved one with a chronic illness or disability is a something few anticipate. The realization that we are responsible for the well-being of a spouse, parent, or even an adult child is a wake-up call to the unpredictability of life. It thrusts family members into roles for which they rarely feel prepared, blurring the lines between personal love and the objective oversight of caregiving and advocacy. When faced with this reality, it's crucial to understand the nature of our role: Are we stepping in as caregivers, advocates, or both?

This chapter explores the complexities and nuances of navigating these roles, emphasizing the importance of effectively recognizing and adapting to them.

The Initial Shock and Role Realization

Many find themselves unexpectedly in the role of a family caregiver, a position born out of necessity rather than choice. At the outset, it's essential to differentiate between being a family caregiver and an advocate. While these roles can overlap and through time and experience, a family caregiver can evolve into an effective advocate; they often start as distinct responsibilities. A family caregiver is typically a relative who provides daily support to their loved one. This support can range from primary supervision to more intensive care, such as bathing, feeding, and managing medications. The bond between the caregiver and the recipient—a "love tie"—motivates this commitment. However, not all caregivers have this emotional connection; sometimes, proximity or circumstance places them in the caregiver role.

The challenge, especially early on, lies in balancing the emotional connection with the practical demands of caregiving. Emotional ties can cloud judgment, making it difficult to act in the best interest of the loved one. The profound impact of seeing a family member in a state of dependency, needing help with the most intimate of tasks, can be emotionally overwhelming. The reversal of roles—from being cared for to being the caregiver—can be a source of significant emotional turmoil.

Understanding this dynamic is the first step in navigating the complexities of caregiving. It's crucial to recognize when emotional responses might hinder the ability to make clear, logical decisions. It's about finding a balance: when to lean into the emotional connection that binds you to your loved one and when to step back and view the situation with a critical, objective eye.

Case Study #1

A sad yet familiar theme played out during a routine check-up visit by a team member from our organization. This story centers on one of our patients who had advanced dementia and her son, who took on the role of her primary caregiver. My team member's visit, by chance, occurred around dinnertime—a moment outside our scheduled care hours—providing a raw and intimate glimpse into the day-to-day reality of their lives. It highlights the complex challenge family caregivers face in balancing their deep love with the need to act as objective advocates.

The son had gone to great lengths to bring a sense of normalcy and comfort to his mother's life despite her advanced dementia. He had ordered her favorite meal—lasagna, garlic bread, and soup—from a beloved restaurant, spending over $70 to have it delivered to their home in hopes of sparking a moment of recognition or joy in her. However, the reality of her condition made this attempt bittersweet.

As he attempted to feed her, it became painfully clear that she no longer recognized him, nor could she engage with her surroundings meaningfully. Her glazed-over eyes and frail demeanor contrasted sharply with the rich, flavorful meal before her—a meal that once might have brought her immense pleasure. Despite his efforts to remind her of the lasagna's significance, coaxing her to eat, she struggled to chew and swallow the food, unable to process what was once familiar. Our team member watched as he painstakingly removed the uneaten food from her mouth.

Navigating caregiving for a loved one with dementia requires balancing the desire to preserve cherished routines with the necessity of adapting to their changing health needs. In this case, the son's well-intentioned efforts to connect with his mother through familiar activities highlight the complexities of being a family caregiver. While his actions were driven by love, they overlooked the importance of tailoring care to her current needs, such as consulting with a speech therapist to evaluate her swallowing capabilities and possibly adjust her diet to ensure her safety and nutrition. This scenario illustrates the crucial role of professional guidance in caregiving, particularly for complex conditions, and the emotional challenges family caregivers face in accepting and adapting to their loved ones' new realities. It's a poignant reminder of the need for both emotional support and objective decision-making in ensuring the safety and well-being of those with dementia.

Case Study #2

Navigating the delicate balance between personal desires and practical needs often challenges family caregivers. This was evident in the case of a client whose husband was living with a severe neurological condition. She deeply valued their intimacy and wished to maintain their routine of sleeping together in their second-floor bedroom despite the logistical nightmares it presented. Her husband, unable to walk unaided and prone to unpredictable spasms, faced significant risks navigating the stairs, even with a stair lift installed. The potential danger of a spasm occurring mid-lift was a constant worry.

Our suggestion to move their bedroom to a more accessible middle level of the house aimed to preserve their closeness while ensuring safety. However, the wife struggled with the idea of altering their long-established sleeping arrangements. Her reluctance wasn't born out of negligence but from a desire to cling to a semblance of normalcy amidst the upheaval caused by her husband's illness. The thought of changing such a fundamental aspect of their daily lives was daunting to her, highlighting the emotional tug-of-war family caregivers face.

Yet, from an advocate's perspective, the priority was clear: ensuring the husband's safety and ability to exit the house quickly in an emergency. An advocate would examine the situation with an eye for minimizing risk, suggesting that sleeping on the first level could significantly enhance safety and accessibility. This scenario illustrates the sometimes-conflicting paths of a caregiver's heartfelt intentions and an advocate's objective, safety-focused approach. This perspective might lead to a checklist to ensure the home environment is optimized for the loved one's mobility and safety.

Accessibility Checklist

Ensuring Clear Paths

> Objective: The main aim is to create an environment where movement is unobstructed, ensuring that pathways within the home are wide open and clear enough to accommodate mobility aids such as wheelchairs or walkers.

Action Steps: Regularly inspect hallways, rooms, and common areas to remove any potential hazards like loose rugs, electrical cords, or furniture that may block the way. Consider the placement of items at a lower level for those with reach limitations and ensure ample space for turning and maneuvering mobility aids.

Accessibility of Exits

> Objective: To facilitate easy exit from the home in case of emergency or for daily activities, ensuring that doors and exit routes are accessible to all, regardless of mobility level.

Action Steps: Evaluate door widths to ensure they comply with accessibility standards and allow wheelchairs to pass easily. Examine thresholds for potential tripping hazards and install ramps where necessary. Consider lever-style door handles that are easier for individuals with limited hand strength or dexterity.

Emergency Preparedness

> Objective: To have a robust plan that addresses the specific needs of individuals with mental or physical challenges during emergencies.

Action Steps: Develop an emergency evacuation plan tailored to the individual's abilities, including clear, accessible escape routes and safe areas to convene outside the home. Make emergency contacts and medical information readily available, and consider registering with local emergency services that offer special assistance for individuals with disabilities.

Stair Navigation

> Objective: To mitigate the risks associated with stair navigation for individuals who find stairs challenging or impossible to use.

Action Steps: Assess the necessity of stair lifts to enable safe ascent and descent, particularly for multi-level homes. Alternatively, reconfigure living spaces to minimize or eliminate the need to use stairs, such as relocating the bedroom to the ground floor. This reduces the risk of falls and promotes greater independence.

Home Safety Modifications

> Objective: To implement modifications throughout the home that increase safety and prevent falls, catering specifically to the unique needs of individuals with physical challenges.

Action Steps: Install grab bars in critical areas like the bathroom and alongside stairs to provide support. Consider using ramps for entry and exit points to ease the transition between levels. Evaluate the need for non-slip flooring to reduce fall risks and ensure adequate lighting throughout the home to improve visibility.

Each of these strategies is designed to make the home safer and enhance the quality of life for individuals with mental or physical challenges. By addressing these key areas, caregivers and advocates can create a living space that is not only functional but also nurturing and inclusive, empowering those they care for to live more independently and with dignity.

Advocacy involves analyzing a situation with a balance of logical consideration and compassionate understanding, prioritizing the well-being and needs of the individual involved over the sway of emotions. While advocates deeply empathize with the challenges at hand, their primary focus remains on identifying and implementing the best possible outcomes for those they represent. This objective perspective is precisely why individuals seek the support of advocates—to have a steadfast ally who offers clear, unbiased guidance. Advocates are adept at navigating through emotional complexities to expedite solutions, always with the individual's best interests at heart, ensuring swift and effective action toward achieving results that are best for the client's mental, physical, and, at times, social well-being.

Case Study# 3

In this case study, we explore the crucial role of advocacy in healthcare through the experience of a woman living in a nursing home. Physically challenged and unable to speak for herself, she found herself in a situation where her desire to return home seemed impossible. Without family or anyone to navigate the healthcare system on her behalf, she was effectively voiceless and trapped within the nursing home's walls.

The turning point came when a friend of hers, though well-intentioned but unfamiliar with the intricacies of healthcare and legal systems, sought external help. Recognizing the need for specialized assistance, the friend contacted me to advocate for the woman.

Upon taking on her case, my first step was communicating directly with her despite her limited ability to speak. The presence of an advocate in healthcare settings like nursing homes can significantly impact the level of attention and care a patient receives. Regular visits and inquiries signal to the staff that the patient is not alone and that an external party is invested in their well-being and quality of care.

To effectively advocate for her, I gathered all the necessary documentation to act on her behalf. This involved detailed discussions with the nursing home administration, her medical team, and rehabilitation specialists to understand her condition, care needs, and the bureaucratic hurdles that needed to be cleared for her to return home.

Critical steps in the advocacy process included obtaining a speech therapy consultation to address her communication challenges, arranging for comprehensive home care services, organizing physician visits to her home, and coordinating home modifications. These modifications, carried out by our organization I-CARE, ensured her home was adapted to meet her physical needs, making it a safe environment for her to live independently.

Within 30 days of my involvement, we transitioned her from the nursing home back to her own home, where she received the necessary support and care. This case highlights the effectiveness of having an advocate who can navigate the healthcare system, leverage a network of resources, and take decisive action to meet a patient's needs. Advocacy goes beyond merely expressing a patient's wishes; it involves a comprehensive approach to overcoming obstacles and ensuring those wishes become a reality. This scenario demonstrates the importance of advocacy in healthcare, particularly for individuals who cannot advocate for themselves due to physical or cognitive limitations.

Blending Family Caregiving with Advocacy

Navigating Ashley's Journey

There are moments when the roles of a family caregiver and an advocate can merge, allowing one to navigate the complex emotional landscape of caring for a loved one while championing their needs with a clear, focused vision. Achieving this dual role doesn't happen overnight; it's the culmination of years immersed in caregiving, where attending countless doctor's appointments, diving deep into research on treatments, insurance, and medications, and building a solid network of healthcare professionals become second nature. This deep involvement enables one to discern the fine line between personal feelings and the critical needs of their loved one, always prioritizing their loved one's well-being above all else, even when it demands tough decisions.

Self-Quiz: Are You a Family Caregiver, an Advocate, or Both?

1. Navigating Medical Complexity

How do you proceed when a new symptom or medical issue arises for your loved one?

Family Caregiver: I provide comfort and possibly look up symptoms online, but I might wait to see if it resolves on its own.

Advocate: I document the symptom, conduct preliminary research, and promptly seek professional consultation to interpret its implications.

Both: I comfort my loved one while taking detailed notes on the symptoms for a professional evaluation, blending emotional support with proactive healthcare navigation.

2. Responding to a Medical Crisis

How do you react if your loved one experiences a sudden health emergency?

Family Caregiver: I may panic or feel overwhelmed but ensure they get to emergency care.

Advocate: I have an emergency plan in place, including who to call and what information to provide to healthcare professionals.

Both: While initial worry is natural, I rely on an established emergency plan, ensuring swift action and informed communication with medical personnel.

3. Engaging with Healthcare Professionals

Describe your interaction with your loved one's healthcare team.

Family Caregiver: I attend appointments but may struggle to ask in-depth questions or challenge medical opinions.

Advocate: I prepare a list of questions and topics for discussion before appointments and am comfortable seeking second opinions.

Both: I attend every appointment with prepared questions and prioritize listening, understanding, and sometimes questioning the care plan to ensure the best outcomes.

4. Making Treatment Decisions

Faced with a significant treatment decision, how do you choose the right path?

Family Caregiver: I might lean heavily on the doctor's recommendations, possibly without fully understanding all options.

Advocate: Before making an informed decision, I research all available treatment options, including potential side effects and impacts on quality of life.

Both: While valuing medical advice, I research independently and consider my loved one's values and quality of life, aiming for a well-informed, balanced decision.

5. Managing Long-term Healthcare Needs

How do you plan for the evolving healthcare needs of your loved one?

Family Caregiver: I focus on day-to-day well-being, sometimes avoiding thinking about the future until necessary.

Advocate: I actively plan for future scenarios, including potential advancements in treatment, changes in condition, and end-of-life care preferences.

Both: I balance daily care with forward-thinking strategies, ensuring current comfort while preparing for future healthcare needs and preferences.

This quiz aims to illuminate the multifaceted roles individuals may play in caring for a loved one. Recognizing your position on this spectrum can empower you to seek additional resources, education, or support to strengthen your advocacy or caregiving capabilities.

Our Journey with Ashley and Multiple Sclerosis

Embracing both roles of family caregiver and advocate presented a significant challenge for me, especially when Ashley fell ill. The initial shock of her diagnosis tested me to my core, yet it also ignited a steadfast determination to fight for her future. My extensive background in healthcare seamlessly bridged my transition from mother to advocate, a journey fraught with emotional highs and lows. My resolve was holding onto hope and trust in the Lord while actively seeking every possible avenue to aid her recovery.

In the following narrative, I aim to delineate the moments where I stood as a family caregiver, stepped up as an advocate, and how the guidance of an external advocate could have streamlined the experience. This reflection is not just a recount of our struggles and victories; it's a testament to the profound impact of embodying love and advocacy in the quest for healing.

In late 2003, we noticed our daughter Ashley had difficulty focusing. She also had back and foot pain that we were trying to correct with orthotics. She was taking challenging courses like Advanced Placement (AP) and college-level Calculus and doing remarkably well in school. She had just applied to a pre-physical therapy program at the University of Miami (UM). We were thrilled when she was accepted, though I felt sad for my baby to leave home.

After Ashley's acceptance to UM, we planned a trip to Florida during her winter break in January 2004 to see the school. Ashley was sluggish during this trip to Florida and did not appear very excited. When we returned home to Virginia, she told me three of her toes felt numb. Initially, I didn't think taking her to the doctor for just a few numb toes was necessary. But the next day, her other foot also exhibited numbness. I then took Ashley to her doctor, who ran blood tests. When the doctor couldn't see any concerning test results, she directed us to have Ashley undergo magnetic resonance imaging (MRI). Along with the MRI, her doctor referred us to a neurologist due to the tingling and numbness in her feet. Having worked at a neurologist's office in the late '80s and watching Ashley's increasing symptoms, I knew the importance of Ashley seeing a neurologist quickly. I called the head neurologist at the office where I had previously been employed, but he was out of town. I knew another neurologist, called his practice, and got Ashley an appointment quickly.

After numerous tests, the neurologist concluded Ashley had Multiple Sclerosis. The doctor described the diagnosis as Ashley's overactive white blood cells triggering inflammation, which then damaged the protective coating of her nerves (called myelin) of her central nervous system (brain and spinal cord). Therefore, the blurred vision, difficulty walking and moving, and numbness and tingling in extremities that Ashley was reporting are all common symptoms of the illness. The neurologist said the images from Ashley's MRI lit up like a Christmas tree, indicating plaque and scarring all over the brain, C-spine, thoracic, lumbar, and sacral spine. He recommended an oral steroid for Ashley's initial treatment to lessen the inflammation.

After Ashley began taking the oral steroid, I could see that it was not helping her enough as her symptoms became worse. She was increasingly unsteady on her feet, had difficulty remembering things, and had trouble with her vision. I called the neurologist and told him I was returning with Ashley. I informed him she needed to be admitted to the hospital, and there needed to be more assessment of her disease course and treatment options. Her cognitive abilities worsened; she forgot the instructions I had just given her. When I asked her to sit down, she obliged me but would get back up after I walked away. From my administrative experience at the neurologist's office, I saw many patients with similar symptoms and recalled their conditions. I again called the neurologist's office and requested a recommendation for a Multiple Sclerosis specialist at Johns Hopkins Hospital in Baltimore. They recommended a neurologist who was the head of Hopkins' Multiple Sclerosis department. As Ashley's mother and advocate, I knew there was no time to waste. It was customary for an appointment with a specialist of this magnitude to take months to secure. However, I used my experience in healthcare and influence in the medical community to advocate for my child. We made an appointment with this specialist within three days.

On the appointment day, Anthony and I drove Ashley two hours to Baltimore, Maryland, for the appointment. We waited patiently as the doctor was full of appointments that day. When we met with the neurologist at Hopkins, he took the time to review all of Ashley's MRIs and test results. He noted the MRI also showed lesions throughout Ashley's brain, C spine, lumbar, sacral, and thoracic regions. He recommended her admittance to the hospital and for her to undergo chemotherapy to slow the progression of the disease and plasma exchange to reduce the inflammation/attack that was happening quickly. The disease was so active in her. Our minds were spinning and overwhelmed. The doctor also said that because the chemotherapy they would use is so powerful, Ashley may not be able to have children in the future. It was therefore mentioned that her eggs could be harvested before beginning the treatment but that harvesting them would delay the treatment of Multiple Sclerosis. This huge decision needed to be made in just hours.

Tony and I decided Ashley's health was the most important thing; she needed to have a future first. We agreed to her beginning the treatment immediately. Our lives changed drastically; we left two teenagers home with neighbors and friends in Virginia. Tony and I committed to being with Ashley during this hospital stay. With the extensive commute, we were offered a room at the Ronald McDonald House affiliated with the hospital. We went back home to collect our other children and stayed there. Ashley was at Hopkins for 14 days for her first treatment.

Ashley continued to have physical and mental struggles with the disease and treatment course, which was thrust upon us with little if any, notice. I researched treatment for MS as well as private jets to fly her to the Mayo Clinic in Rochester, Minnesota. I refused to give up or despair. I was determined to find out precisely what was wrong and how to treat her. When her first six-month round of chemotherapy ended, the team at Hopkins discovered Ashley had nine new lesions on her brain and spinal cord. Even one of the neurologists said, "We just really don't know what we're going to do." I would not accept his utterance of defeat; I held onto my faith and pressed onwards.

Through my research and speaking with Ashley's physicians, I learned that Multiple Sclerosis could worsen over time. However, early in Ashley's treatment, there was one doctor who told me, "This is the best time to have Multiple Sclerosis." When he said this, I looked at Tony and said... What did he say? Our daughter had lesions throughout her brain and entire spinal region, multiple hospitalizations, medication treatments, and traveling to numerous neurologists in the tri-state region. And this was the best time for MS? After the initial shock by his statement, I understood his perspective to be true. Due to limited treatments and information about this illness, an MS diagnosis before 1990 often meant patients were debilitated for life. Thanks to new technology and medications, an MS patient's outlook was much better in 2004, when Ashley was diagnosed. Ashley's youth, faith, and support system were also advantageous to her improvement.

Tony and I clung to our faith in Christ and relied on his promises. Hope was the thread that was now keeping our family together. Tony would tell Ashley things were going to get better next year. Caring for Ashley became my life's work for the time. I stayed with her for most of her numerous hospitalizations, bringing my computer and bags with me to make sure I was available for the midnight doctor's visits and could answer and ask questions about Ashley's condition when she was not able to do so. I had to push the doctors to do what they said was impossible.

My diligence and tenacity helped my daughter receive the care she needed. Ashley was hospitalized 42 times in her first three years with MS, and she endured more than 100 hospitalizations overall. I had a pleasant yet persistent demeanor and interacted with others, merging my mothering care with my business acumen to pursue and convey the outcome necessary for her benefit. Even when our insurance company refused to pay for Ashley to see a neuro-ophthalmologist for her vision impairments, I fought through endless phone calls until the treatment was covered. My determination took aback many doctors, and I believe they took notice of it and went the extra mile for Ashley in her care.

There were terrifying moments in our fight against the disease. We later discovered one of the reasons why Ashley had so many hospitalizations was her susceptibility to infection from her hospital stays. Infection is not a friend of MS. Once an MS patient becomes ill, the white blood cells increase their activity to fight the infection, triggering even more inflammation. Doctors call this an MS relapse. The doctors would treat the MS flare-up with steroids to reduce inflammation, but the steroids would feed the infection. What a vicious cycle to endure.

My daughter was in the intensive care unit three times because she had life-threatening extreme reactions to infections called sepsis. We could be anywhere when Ashley had a relapse due to infection. We could be at home, at church, shopping, or down the street, and then Ashley would have a relapse. We took her straight to the hospital and sat in the emergency room. I even employed one of our caregivers at I-CARE to work with Ashley during a relapse when Tony and I were out of town or otherwise unavailable. The caregiver would take Ashley to the hospital and care for Ashley as I would have if I could have been there. It would take a few weeks of patience, persistence, and movement therapies, but after relapses, Ashley's functions would return.

During one hospitalization, Ashley was at Georgetown Hospital because she experienced a movement disorder related to MS called Paroxysmal Kinesigenic Dyskinesia (or PKD). It was unlike anything I had ever seen. Her hands would turn in, her face would become distorted, and she would curl up and convulse. Watching her convulsions were some of the scariest moments of my life. At the time, the doctors at Georgetown didn't understand Ashley's inability to control these episodes. Again, we advocated for her proper and appropriate care. What's more, the doctors told me these convulsions were her "new normal," but neither Tony, Ashley, nor I were prepared to accept such a prognosis.

Ashley was confined to a bed, unable to sit up or move on her own. The doctors focused on small goals, like getting her to sit up on the edge of the bed. But my daughter had bigger aspirations. She wanted to walk out of the hospital in heels, and with determination and hard work, she did.

Over time, Ashley was prescribed various medications to try to stop the convulsions. However, she believed the medications affected her strangely, so she stopped taking them. Doctors then wanted to put morphine in her baclofen pump, but my daughter refused. She didn't want to live with a drip of morphine all the time. She told us all the medications made her mind move slowly. As scared as we were for her, Tony and I had to trust Ashley when she said some of these medications did her more harm than good. She reduced taking some medications to manage the MS symptoms, and we explored some alternative ways to complement the complete treatment plan to combat Ashley's condition. Within a year, we decided we would use an aggressive treatment to combat the white blood cells that were attacking her nervous system. We wanted to get to the "heart of the matter" instead of the many medications to treat symptoms.

Each of us began undergoing psychotherapy, which had a significant impact on our family's mental and emotional health. I firmly believe it is essential to see both a doctor and a mental health specialist when dealing with any health issue. One psychotherapist uniquely encouraged Ashley and our family to think about having MS differently. He encouraged us to see Ashley as someone who may have symptoms instead of assuming MS as her identity. This shift allowed Ashley to experience life and not let her diagnosis become a burden. She could approach her condition respectfully while living her life to the fullest. Through the years, she began to accept her condition, choose prudent treatment, make lifestyle changes, and embrace her life as a gift to be cherished.

Despite this trial being the most challenging one our family had faced, we had faith that things would get better. My faith in God grew exponentially during Ashley's health struggles. As I reflect on the 20 years since her initial MS diagnosis, I see I had to rely on Him instead of relying on myself.

Eventually, things did get better. Her relapses occurred less frequently, and her functions improved. My daughter's strength and brilliance shone radiantly; she continues to learn to advocate for herself but knows when to call on me when necessary. Ashley is determined not to let Multiple Sclerosis or her past struggles with the disease define her. Even amid seemingly insurmountable challenges, she persevered and accomplished much the doctors said she could not. Ashley continues to defeat the odds of her initial prognosis, even to the point of the doctors stating that due to the intense chemotherapy, she probably would not be able to have children. We are eternally grateful that Ashley is a mother of two beautiful children.

Ashley's diagnosis of Multiple Sclerosis was a significant event that reshaped our family dynamics and the operational ethos of I-CARE. This experience taught us that illness doesn't only affect the individual; it touches everyone connected to them, influencing relationships, daily routines, and the overall well-being of the family unit. This insight motivated us to refine our personal and professional approach, ensuring that our work at I-CARE reflects the depth of support families need when facing health challenges. This realization propelled us, Tony and I, to adapt and evolve not just in our personal lives but in our professional mission, and it defined the actual reason Why I-CARE.

Closing Thoughts

And as much human effort as one can put into life, never lose faith in God or His power to work miracles. I never thought or dreamt I could run a company, let alone a thriving one. I started I-CARE with no business experience and a Montgomery Ward credit card. I was a shy childhood introvert, not a confident businesswoman. But I trusted in God's plan and allowed Him to guide me. He carried me through life's trials and tribulations. I couldn't have done it alone. He taught me the lessons of my life education. Sometimes, the lessons were easy to accept; sometimes, I fought them but ultimately believed his way to be the best. I am living proof of the power of faith and God's ability and sufficiency.

Part Two

Ashley's Story

Introduction

Early Beginnings

Faith, Family, Strive for Excellence, I-CARE

My father came from a large Methodist family with 10 children, and his parents instilled in him the importance of a deep and abiding faith in Christ. He became a Christian as a teenager, and he was a foundational influence in my mother's life and her putting her faith in Christ, too.

When I was young, I didn't fully understand my parents' faith. I saw their routine of attending church, but I didn't know why they spent so much time there. My family and I were incredibly involved in our church and attended weekly activities. On Monday evenings, there was tutoring. My mom insisted that we stay for tutoring until we achieved an A in each subject. Once we did, we would help tutor others struggling in school.

Tuesday evenings, choir practice; Wednesdays, Bible study and prayer meeting; Thursdays, choir practice or usher meetings; Fridays, spiritual bowling (yes, it's a thing); Saturdays, whatever still needed practicing; and Sundays were for services. Church started as early as 7:45 A.M. and lasted sometimes until 2:00 P.M. Church was our second home. Such was the life of the Ivey kids: we were either at home, school, work, or church. The church was a fun place to go and where I could hang out with my friends. Growing up in a predominantly African American church, I also learned to appreciate my heritage, my skin, my facial features, and culture. I memorized scripture and learned many biblical stories, but at the time, it just remained knowledge. My parents' teachings, my church's sermons, and my reading of the Bible, however, did lay a foundation for me to truly rely on God in faith in hard times and trust Him as my Savior.

I am the oldest of three children; my younger sister, April, was born when I was two years old, and my brother, Anthony, is almost five years younger than I am. Since April and I are so close in age, I don't remember life without her. I do, however, remember life before my little brother, Anthony. It was just April and I, playing with or fighting over baby dolls, getting all the fun and attention from my parents. But then, my little brother happened, and I recall going to the hospital when my brother was born. My sister and I sat in the waiting area with a family friend, awaiting his birth. I was excited then; however, when we came home, April and I quickly realized Anthony Jr. was now the center of attention. He was an adorable, curly-haired baby with a beautiful smile, and he was the only son in the family. The newness and excitement for April and I wore off quickly. I am sure I asked my parents if we could take him back to wherever he came from.

We moved to a close-knit community in Burke, Virginia, when I was 10 years old, and I spent most of my youth there. Our neighborhood was picturesque, and our house was on a big corner lot with a large yard. My siblings and I had friends in the neighborhood, and we would spend time in the Summer and evenings playing with them until it got dark outside.

My father sowed in us the seeds of discipline in the large and small things. As an example, he prioritized having a clean home. He was a stickler for cleanliness and took pride in keeping everything spotless. If you look in my dad's closet today, all his clothes are perfectly organized by type and color. My mom would also teach us kids how to make cleaning a game or make it fun by singing a song while we cleaned. From washing dishes, wiping counters, or vacuuming the floors, we learned quickly that we were a vital part of maintaining our household. As kids, we were to memorize a verse of Scripture every day, and we recited them to Dad at the beginning of our family dinners each evening. He kept us accountable and motivated us to pursue excellence. I admire my father's discipline, and it has served me well in my own life. As an adult, I recognize my day requires preparation and effort. I wake up at 4:00 A.M. to exercise, meditate, and pray before my day begins at 6:00 A.M.

My mother, too, kept us accountable for our education. No matter what her day entailed, she attended every parent-teacher conference and gave our teachers her business card. I remember hearing her heels clicking down our school hallways and her keys jingling. She invited our teachers to call her for anything they needed, and she meant it. She would also instruct us to use proper grammar in speaking and writing. She would charge us money any time we spoke improperly or misspelled. We would then have to dig under the couch cushions for loose change. I sometimes asked my dad for a dollar when he came home. She was serious about our payments and wanted her money on time. My mom also encouraged friendly competition at home to see who could read the most books during school breaks. She found many ways to make education fun and challenging for us.

My parents gave us a valuable tool in teaching us to care for ourselves and others. They gave us responsibilities and tasks that were increasingly difficult as we aged. One of my funniest childhood recollections is when my parents showed us as teenagers how to cook. We learned kitchen safety and the use of all kitchen tools and appliances. My parents trusted us to do our jobs well, and we each became strong in our skills. But there was no cross-training! My brother would help my dad make breakfast on the weekends, my sister would create the desserts, and I would cook the meals. We each had our specialty, but we never really learned how to do the others' jobs. For me, this still holds to this day. I cook beautiful meals but can't bake to save my life! My parents encouraged us to develop our expertise in the kitchen. Their instruction served each of us by imparting a valuable life skill; for me, cooking became a passion and a way of expressing love. I stick to making breakfast, lunch, and dinner, and there I shine.

When my mom began I-CARE Inc. in 1993, she only had a computer and a passion. My parents empowered us children to grow in our professional skills at a young age. They instilled a strong work ethic and emphasized the importance of pursuing all tasks with excellence. We have also carried these skills with us to adulthood. Over time, our family became one with our family business, I-CARE Inc., which provides home health care to patients needing personal caregiving and nursing services. It truly is a family business.

At our home in Burke, my father used his construction management background to convert our large basement into office space. We had everything we needed. At 8:00 A.M., we greeted staff arriving with their coffees and smiles. My mom reminded us that our home was also a place of business, and we should care for it accordingly. For example, she would not fry chicken or fish for our Sunday dinners. She did not want the smell to linger until the next day.

We have never known anything different; I-CARE Inc. has been a big part of our lives. We are all invested in its success. My siblings and I began working for I-CARE Inc. at age 14; we joked we received a birthday cake and a worker's permit. I had watched my parents work hard from my youth, but at younger ages, I did not understand why they did so. Working with them at I-CARE gave me an appreciation for their dedication. I undertook administrative tasks such as typing notes, sending invoices, and keeping records. When I-CARE began, we provided rehabilitation services to our clients. One of my jobs was to refer to the therapists' notes and maintain all the data. Another task was to compile invoices and input the corresponding notes to ensure payment and verify accuracy. It is incredible to think my parents trusted me with such responsibility. They knew they had trained me well. They believed I could do a great job.

One day, when I was in a rush to leave work, I still had some invoices to send. So, I quickly put them all into an envelope and addressed it. However, when my dad checked my work and saw the envelope, he pointed out that it did not look very professional. In my haste, I had written the name and address diagonally across the envelope. He reminded me our work reflects the business, and he wanted to present I-CARE Inc. as best we could. Dad asked me to redo the envelope Doing things correctly the first time is crucial because it saves time, money and effort. As my brother says, "It is expensive being cheap." This experience taught me to take pride in my work and to contribute meaningfully as part of a team.

My mom was a stickler for putting forth our best efforts. When I was about 15 or 16, my mom wrote me a warning letter for breaking the office dress code. At the time, we could only wear jeans on Fridays. Since I was going downstairs to the basement office, I thought I could get away with it. But my mom caught me and held me to the same standard as all her employees. She could have let it go since I am her daughter, but she believed having a professional appearance and demeanor was essential for every team member, including her children. She also instructed me, "Smile; they can hear it through the phone." It reflects well on our organization when the staff is cheerful and courteous. I continue to work for I-CARE Inc. as a clinical manager and a physical therapy assistant. Around a year ago, one patient remarked he could hear me smiling through the phone. He told me how much my infusing hope in a difficult situation meant to him.

Watching my parents interact and work together is inspiring. My mom is the visionary behind the business; I call her "the balloon." She is full of ideas, and her ideas soar. She is the company's heart, a servant at her core, and always willing to help others. I call my dad "the string" of the business. He excels in the business aspect of I-CARE® Inc. and is the grounding force for our endeavors. People often ask what it is like working with my parents. I respond, "It is amazing!" We work exceptionally well together. They are a fantastic duo, and I believe I have inherited a bit of both of their characteristics. I am a mix of their dedicated commitment and pragmatic business attitudes. We have fun together, we support each other, and we make sure to prioritize our family above all else. My mom, dad, and I utilize our unique giftings to brainstorm how to help more patients or to better our services. We also pray and ask God's guidance before making our decisions. We entrust our lives and this business to Him.

My parents, with their deep faith and hard work ethic, always led by example. They showed us the importance of discipline, from keeping the house clean to doing well in school, and they made sure we were involved in church and learned to rely on God. Working for I-CARE from a young age taught me responsibility and gave me a firsthand look at the healthcare world, which was incredibly valuable later on.

When I think about it, I'm struck by how everything seems to have a purpose. My parents started a healthcare company, my mom's experience in the field, and even my getting sick – it doesn't feel like a coincidence. It feels like God was preparing us all along, equipping us with the faith, the family bonds, and the practical skills we'd need. It's a reminder of how God works in our lives, often in ways we don't understand at the time but that makes sense when we look back.

WHY I-CARE & WHY I-CARE TOO

Hello, I am Ashley Ivey. Welcome to 'Why I-CARE. Too'

Chapter 5

Beyond the Diagnosis
Finding Strength in Struggle

Embracing my life and who God has called me to be has taught me to appreciate every moment of my life, including the tough times. I'm excited to share what I've learned, especially from living with a chronic illness. In the first part of this book, my mother, Donna Ivey, speaks about how God intricately arranged life's twists and turns, positioning her to become an exemplary advocate. From her early childhood, through working in health care at the neurology center to starting her own home health care company, I-CARE, each gave her the tools, experience, and resources she needed to care for me when I was diagnosed with MS.

As we transition from my mother's narrative to mine, expect a shift in tone and perspective. My mother's advocacy and insights form a comprehensive view of healthcare from both the provider's and the patient's perspective.

My story delves deeply into the patient experience and my personal struggle with MS. It chronicles the profound impact the initial diagnosis had on every facet of my life, from altering my physical abilities to reshaping my social interactions and professional aspirations. The aim of my part of the book is twofold: to connect with those navigating similar health challenges, giving hope and tangible strategies that I call my secret sauce to success, that I have and to offer guidance to families and caregivers striving to understand and support their loved ones that are going through a chronic illness.

I hope to provide practical insights and encouragement by sharing my "secret sauce"—the strategies that have allowed me to manage MS and maintain mobility against the odds. Let's be clear, this is not a "how I overcame" story. I have not reached the summit; I am still climbing. I still live with MS, and I continue to follow my medical, mental health, physical health, and nutritional health routine to keep the relapses at bay. Over time, I began to find strength in my unique circumstances. I realized that my experiences with MS, though different, offered a perspective that was uniquely mine. I started to embrace my challenge, understanding that it could inspire others facing similar struggles. The last 20 years with Multiple Sclerosis (MS) haven't been easy, but it taught me the importance of perseverance and the power of hope. Through my experiences, I've come to appreciate the minor victories and the beauty in everyday moments. I have also learned and continue to embrace these valuable lessons: There is purpose in pain, strength in a struggle, and an incredible power we possess to live life despite adversity. In sharing my story, I hope to offer hope to others, showing that even in the face of challenges, it's possible to carve out a fulfilling, meaningful, and amazing life.

Triple Insight: Navigating Healthcare from Every Angle

Having spent 24 years in healthcare administration and management, 14 years as a clinician, and 20 years living with Multiple Sclerosis, I've seen the healthcare world from nearly every angle. My upbringing in the family business, I-CARE, instilled in me the values of compassion and caregiving from an early age. This background is more than a part of my work history; it's deeply intertwined with my personal story. I've played multiple roles within our company, I-CARE, from handling administrative tasks and providing care to receiving care during MS flare-ups. These varied experiences have equipped me with a comprehensive outlook on the integral aspects of healthcare.

As a clinician, I've experienced the challenges patients face, from serious health conditions to the struggle of losing independence. Having been on the receiving end of care, I know what it's like to be in the patient's shoes, relying on others for help. Now, as one of the people running I-CARE, I try to see the full picture, blending my experiences to serve better as a clinician, be more understanding as an administrator, and be more cooperative as a patient.

Often, people say, "Was it odd or was it God?" pondering whether the purposeful and orderly alignment of events in life is mere coincidence or the work of a divine hand? Looking back at my life, I know unequivocally it is God.

I-CARE, started by my parents, has always been more than just a job to me. It's taught me to value helping and caring for others above all. This grounding and my own personal healthcare experience have helped me appreciate the complex needs of healthcare from every perspective – knowing what patients go through, understanding the demands on clinicians, and the intricacies of running a healthcare business. I've learned to navigate the business side of healthcare, understanding the behind-the-scenes operations that make everything tick. As a clinician, I've been up close with patients' challenges, from severe health conditions to the struggle of losing independence. And having been on the receiving end of care, I know what it's like to be in the patient's shoes, relying on others for help. Whether dealing with patient care or the administrative side, I aim to bring empathy, understanding, and a willingness to see things from all sides. It's about combining my roles to be more effective – a better clinician, a more empathetic boss, and a patient who understands the effort to help me heal.

Living with Grace: A Journey of Poetry and Resilience Through MS

The beginning of this book is deliberately thorough. I first give an overview of who I am and how I grew up so that you can see how God's handiwork was preparing us for what would become my life with MS. The next chapter illustrates the profound impact the MS diagnosis and subsequent health struggles had on my life. It delves into the physical constraints imposed by the disease, its social consequences, and the effect my illness had on my parents and younger siblings. The purpose is to set the foundation showing where I was and how these experiences shaped my perspective, offering a comprehensive view of the challenges I encountered and the triumphs that have ultimately defined me.

In my early 20s, at the beginning of my bout with MS, I wished there was a simple guide for dealing with the disease, something solid to hold onto during all the uncertainty. But what I encountered was a mix of advice, from bee sting therapy to specific prayers to say at specific times of the day for healing to doing intensive medications and experimental treatments, none of which truly resonated with me. So now, I'm sharing a look back at what has genuinely helped me, hoping to offer guidance to others facing similar challenges. After the introduction and the groundwork about the MS diagnosis, we start having fun in the rest of the book! I delve into what I affectionately term my "secret sauce"—the amalgamation of practices, beliefs, and actions that have not only sustained me through two decades since my MS diagnosis but have also enabled me to defy expectations. Despite predictions that I would require assistive devices for mobility within a decade of my diagnosis, I am thankful to navigate life today, 20 years post-diagnosis, without them, even walking in heels. Thank you, Lord.

Poetry has become my sanctuary, helping me to express those parts of living with MS that are hard to put into words. Everything started to click into place when I wove my thoughts into poetry, using metaphor and rhyme. That's why you'll find poetry throughout my part of this book. It became my way of clearly expressing the complex emotions and experiences I faced with my illness. However, poetry wasn't just a creative outlet; it was a lifeline that helped me articulate the depth of my struggles and has been a way for me to share the subtleties of what I'm going through, making things more straightforward for my doctors. For instance, when I was in my early 20s, one of my doctors couldn't grasp a particular symptom I was experiencing. I was struggling to explain the intense lower back pain I felt, so I turned to poetry, crafting lines filled with imagery to convey the pain. After sharing the poem with my doctor, he finally understood what I was describing and was able to offer a better treatment plan. In my part of the book, you'll find various poems I've written, each one capturing feelings and situations that seemed too complex or elusive for plain language. Using metaphors and rhymes has helped me piece together my thoughts and emotions in a way that feels complete.

If you are reading this as a patient, you may be able to relate to some of the poems; if you are reading this as an advocate of a family member of a patient, I pray that the poems help you understand how it feels to be "sick" and have the life you knew change in insurmountable ways. It was predicted that within a decade, I would likely be bound to a wheelchair or dependent on a cane or walker for mobility. However, I knew that I was more than a diagnosis and more than the limitations it sought to impose. My MS journey continues to compel me to discover inner strengths, to learn the art of finding joy in the smallest victories, and to embrace life's unpredictability with faith. Reflecting on the past two decades living with MS, I have come to appreciate that our greatest challenges can create our most profound strengths.

Chapter 6

MS

Two Letters That Were the Turning Point in My Life

Diagnosis Day- It was a day like any other, except it wasn't. Twenty years ago, sitting in a sterile doctor's office, on the precipice of adulthood, I was about to hear two letters that would change my life. I was 18 years old and filled with dreams and aspirations typical of someone my age. Just three weeks earlier, I had been basking in the excitement of being accepted into my dream school, the University of Miami. Thoughts of college life filled my mind – a blend of freedom, fun, and the sun-kissed beaches of Coral Gables, Florida. But in a single, life-altering consultation, those dreams were cast into a churning sea of uncertainty. The doctor, with a tone blending routine medical professionalism and clinical detachment, looked at me and said, "Ashley, it looks like you have MS." Those words, seemingly simple, echoed profoundly in the space, marking the beginning of a life path I never anticipated.

Ok... so what exactly is that? I thought to myself. These words from my doctor, laden with a diagnosis I barely comprehended, felt distant, as though they were meant for someone else, someone a lot older than me. At 18, I had only heard the term MS used a couple of times when I was at work or watching TV. My parents own a home healthcare agency that, at the time, focused on physical, occupational, and speech therapy staffing services. One of my daily work tasks was to check patients' therapy notes and ensure that the documentation had the proper information: Name of client, name of a therapist, clock in and out time, signature from client, therapist, and diagnosis. I had occasionally seen the term "MS" listed as the diagnosis of "elderly" patients who were receiving therapy. At age 18, I naively considered "elderly" anyone who was over the age of 40. Additionally, I recall once catching a bit of the Montell Williams show during a school break. Lounging at home, eager to indulge in the world of daytime television, I had been channel surfing when I stumbled upon his show in which he was describing his personal battles with MS. The topic, foreign and seemingly irrelevant to my carefree teen life, failed to hold my interest.

I quickly switched channels to something I thought was way more entertaining, "The Price Is Right", not realizing how significant MS would become in my life.

Now, the term MS, was suddenly, jarringly personal. It was no longer just an acronym on a therapy note or a topic on a daytime talk show; it was a diagnosis being directed at me, an 18-year-old with her entire life ahead of her. Never had I imagined that this distant medical term would become a central character in my own life story.

The Unraveling of Normal

As I sat in the cold, sterile office, my mind grappled with the definition the doctor gave us for Multiple Sclerosis. MS – a chronic, progressively debilitating disease where the body's immune system attacks the protective sheath (myelin) that covers nerve fibers, causing communication problems between the brain and the rest of the body. This definition, impersonal, clinical, and filled with medical jargon, offered a glimpse into the profound impact it would have on my life. The worst part of it is that it offered no glimmer of hope.

As I sat in the doctor's office, I found it hard to keep up with the information he was sharing with me. The doctor spoke about treatment plans, the expected progression of the disease, and management strategies, but my thoughts were clouded with confusion and disbelief. Despite my efforts to focus on what he was saying, my attention kept drifting towards my toes. They were still tingly. The tingling was constant but wouldn't have bothered me as much if that was the only issue I was dealing with. A week or so before this visit, I was headed to 3rd-period Spanish class at my high school when I impulsively took off my shoes right in the middle of the hallway. As bizarre as it was, I was convinced there were cotton balls in the middle of each of my toes. I knew that I had not placed cotton balls in between my toes that morning as I was getting ready for school, but still, the sensation was so real and felt so intense I had to check. I took off my shoes and my socks, and sure enough, there was nothing tangible in between my toes. I placed my index finger in between each toe, and I was shocked at what I felt.

Nothing.

My fingers could feel my toes, but my toes did not feel my fingers' touch. Slightly scared, I wiggled my toes; I could barely feel the movement.

As my attention was brought back to the doctor's office, I heard him describing some sort of treatment plan. I listened to him talk to my mom, who had accompanied me to the appointment. He detailed steps and procedures in a tone that suggested routine, but to me, it felt anything but ordinary. Once again, my mind shifted. This time, to my belly, it was still numb. The numbness had stealthily claimed my abdomen, rendering it totally absent of sensation. These weren't merely symptoms; they were the harbingers of a new reality.

Sitting on the cold exam table, I looked at the doctor. There was a white, hazy outline on his face, and it was hard to distinguish any of his facial features. I blinked and blinked again. The blurriness in my eyes had gotten worse. I looked at my mom sitting in the doctor's office with me. Her presence, once a source of unspoken security, now mirrored the gravity of my situation. It was a poignant realization - my struggle with MS wasn't mine alone; it was shared with my family, silently shouldering the weight of my diagnosis.

I couldn't make out my mom's facial features, but I could read her body language. It expressed readiness, as if life had been subtly but purposefully shaping her for this very moment. Dressed in her business attire, her hair perfectly styled, and makeup meticulously applied - she was the epitome of preparedness. It was as if God had placed her life experience to culminate in this moment, equipping her with an unwavering strength to face the unknowns of my diagnosis. Her readiness was not just in her attire but in her entire being. Her poised demeanor, contrasting with the confusion I felt inside, was a silent promise of hope.

In the doctor's office, enveloped by the clinical atmosphere of medical formality, my mother and I sat side by side. I felt vulnerable and filled with uncertainty, while my mother appeared steadfast and prepared. Together, we faced the onset of a journey that promised to test our faith, and the resilience of our family's love in ways we could have never comprehended.

Everything changed on the "diagnosis day" of February 19, 2004. At the age of 18, I was diagnosed with an aggressive relapsing-remitting form of Multiple Sclerosis. The life I had envisioned – college freedoms, adventures, first love – seemed to crumble under the weight of my new reality.

MS traded my idea of easily coasting through the last four months of high school with a barrage of limiting MS symptoms and hospitalizations. It exchanged my anticipated freshman year of college for a grueling regimen of chemotherapy and painful treatments. MS traded my high heels for the constrained mobility of a wheelchair. All of this without my permission. I just wanted to be normal again. I just wanted to be me.

To Be Me
A poem by Ashley Ivey

Breath in and breath out,
Seems simple, but I doubt

It will make me feel any better.

The tragedy of simplicity
Is that it doesn't see the complexity
Of my pain.

From top to bottom, inside through
I hurt, I'm distraught,
If you only knew

The plans that I had
The almost-reached dreams
The excitement for life
My eager heart beams.

Snatched away,

Taken,

Without warning.
No breath in my lungs
My mind, soul mourning.

To take a breath seemed like such a breeze
When life was calm and at ease.

But now,
How can I even think to inhale,
When all systems stutter and start to fail?

How do I press to take a stand?
When life is determined to be unplanned?

How do I part my eyes to see
When life suffocates completely?

Breaks me

WHY I-CARE & WHY I-CARE TOO

Takes me

Hurts me

And Offers NO APOLOGIES!

How can I move when my legs don't approve?

How do I climb when my hands can't find
Where they should go next?

I am perplexed.
Confused
Heart abused.

I'm hurting, why can't you see?
My yearn to be "normal,"
I just want to be me.

My First MS Symptoms

The first MS symptom that I can remember happened 6 months before the diagnosis.

On a hot summer day in 2003, during a seemingly ordinary church trip from Virginia to an amusement park in Maryland, I encountered an experience that was anything but normal. It was a perfect day for fun – sunny, with lots of laughter and excitement. My sister and I were immersed in the thrill of the amusement rides, running from one rollercoaster to the next. But then, out of nowhere, my legs just stopped working. I couldn't move them at all. I was, trying to get to the next ride, and suddenly, it was like my legs were on a break without telling me. I felt both confused and embarrassed. There I was, amid all the fun, suddenly finding myself stuck in place, unable to take even a single step. As the sun continued to beam down on me, I could hear my sister calling out, urging me to hurry up and join her. Yet, my legs were unresponsive

My sister and I were all about hitting as many rides as we could. She thought I was messing around, but I was seriously stuck. It felt like forever, standing there, trying to get my legs to listen to me. I even started talking to them, hoping somehow that would kick start them into action. It was a mix of frustration and fear, not understanding what was going on with my own body. It seemed like hours, although only minutes passed, but my legs finally decided to cooperate, and I could walk again. We just carried on with our day, getting on more rides and having fun, and I pushed that weird moment to the back of my mind.

In the fall of 2003, I was in my senior year of high school, juggling a demanding schedule filled with Advanced Placement classes and language courses, including a dive into the world of Calculus. Despite my initial indifference towards math, Calculus started off well, and I found myself surprisingly good at it. However, as the semester progressed, my once firm grasp on the material began to slip, and retaining information became harder and harder to do. My grade in Calculus took a nosedive from the start to the end of the first semester, which was alarming enough to prompt my mom to talk to my school counselor. Surprised by this sudden drop, she requested that I be withdrawn from the class and have it marked as incomplete to avoid impacting my GPA. Since I had already fulfilled my high school math requirements and this class was extra, she thought it was the best move. Moreover, with my college application to the University of Miami pending, she didn't want this unexpected slump in my grades to jeopardize my admission. So, we went ahead with that plan, and I dropped the class. Still, I was left feeling shocked and somewhat puzzled about why remembering steps and processes was becoming increasingly difficult for me.

Then, something amazing happened that pushed that academic struggle to to the side. Just six days after my 18th birthday, on January 15, 2004, I received the best news ever—I got into the University of Miami, my dream college. I was beyond happy. Not only was this an amazing school and one of the leading schools for Physical Therapy in the nation (the career I wanted to pursue), but this was a feat my high school counselor said would be very hard for me to do. She said that since I only had a 3.3 GPA, I would probably not get into the University of Miami because of expected from incoming Freshmen. Her doubt inspired me to go home, complete my application, write an amazing essay, get academic references, and submit my application to the University of Miami early. Now, I was sitting there with the confirmation that I had been accepted. My counselor's doubt pushed me to work harder to achieve my goals.

My family and I were beyond happy; you could really feel the excitement and pride in the air. Two weeks after I received my acceptance letter, my parents surprised me with a trip to visit the University of Miami in Coral Gables, Florida. I was thrilled for a couple of reasons. First, I couldn't wait to check out the campus, especially since my dad mentioned he'd be putting down a deposit. That was his way of saying, "Yes, you're really going!" And second, I was just happy to escape the cold. We left Virginia in the middle of an ice storm, and a few hours later, we landed in the warm, sunny world of Coral Gables. Seeing palm trees and feeling the warm sun after leaving the icy cold was amazing.

The whole trip to the University of Miami was great. We toured the school, purchased UM apparel, a sweatshirt, and a cup, and my dad paid the deposit. Nothing could have made me happier. On our way back to the airport to come back to Virginia, I was seriously on cloud 9. Little did I know, this trip would mark both my first and final visit to Coral Gables, Florida.

When we arrived back in Virginia, we landed in a snowstorm. It was cold and icy outside. It's amazing how drastically the weather can change in just a 2-and-a-half-hour plane ride. A few days after returning home from Florida, I noticed a strange tingling sensation in the last three toes of my left foot. Initially, I thought it was a minor issue, but the tingling gradually became more persistent, and I couldn't ignore it any longer. I spoke with my mother about the problem, and she suggested that I keep an eye on it. She also advised me to let her know if the tingling sensation started to spread to my other foot. That is exactly what happened. The exact same tingling that I felt in my toes on the left foot, I started to feel in my toes on my right foot. Within the next few days, I started feeling numb around my waist and my vision got blurry. I started losing my balance, and I was walking so strangely that my sister thought I was messing around. It was the start of a huge change in my life. At school, I kept falling asleep in class, I couldn't stay awake in class no matter how much rest I received the night before. My teachers noticed and talked to me about being more attentive. The next Sunday, I didn't feel good so I asked my parents if I could stay at home. They said yes, and I went back to bed to rest. I woke up feeling dizzy and confused. As I was trying to go to my bedroom door, I fell and threw up. I had no clue what was going on. I called my mom on my cell phone and told her what happened. She then started the process of calling her contacts and doctors to get me seen. It took approximately nine months from the time of my first symptom (at the amusement park) until now. The symptoms were diverse and odd on their own, but when considered together, they showed the subtle but relentless way Multiple Sclerosis (MS) came into my life.

Reshaping of My Life

The diagnosis and symptoms of Multiple Sclerosis didn't merely interrupt my life; it demanded a complete and relentless reshaping of it. It was an unwelcome author rewriting my story, erasing my plans, and redrafting my dreams. The simplicity of being a "normal" teenager, once taken for granted, became a conscious effort. My aspirations and my excitement for the future felt as though they had been snatched away without warning.

The MRI scans of my brain and spinal cord painted an unambiguous picture. Lesions were scattered across my central nervous system; brain, cervical, thoracic and lumbar spinal cord. The lumbar puncture confirmed what the MRIs had shown, and the results of both visual and auditory evoked potentials didn't leave much room for doubt. However, I naively held on to the belief that Multiple Sclerosis (MS) was a temporary intruder in my life, something that would eventually go away like a bad cold. It was February 2004, a time when my focus should have been on wrapping up my final high school classes and looking forward to college in the fall. But soon after the diagnosis of MS, the disease forced a dramatic and quick shift in my plans that I was not ready for.

Despite the increasing frequency of hospital visits, various treatments, and a growing list of physical challenges - from walking difficulties to blurred vision and memory lapses, I clung to the belief that I would still attend University of Miami for college that fall. The reality of not attending college that year, a future I had so meticulously planned, seemed a distant, almost irrelevant thought. Despite my optimistic but naive denial, reality soon set in. As my functions and health deteriorated rapidly, I realized that MS was not a temporary guest.

After the diagnosis, the initial treatment was oral steroids at home. However, their effectiveness was short-lived and within a week, my condition worsened, prompting my mother to seek further medical intervention. This marked the beginning of what would become a routine part of my life - hospitalizations. Over the next three years, I was admitted to the hospital over 42 times for MS relapses and worsening symptoms. MS relapses are heightened inflammation of the brain and spinal cord lesions, disrupting nerve signals and causing many debilitating symptoms. My life oscillated between periods of intense symptoms - numbness, mobility issues, vision problems, difficulty swallowing, and sensory challenges in my hands - and brief respites of recovery. However, the recoveries I had were so remarkable that they frequently wiped away any signs of the relapse ever occurring. Nevertheless, during the initial three years of living with MS, the relief brought by quick recoveries was always overshadowed by the anticipation of the next relapse.

When you're diagnosed with a significant illness, the immediate focus tends to be on the disease itself. But as time goes on, you start to realize how it impacts every aspect of your life. In my life, it wasn't just about grappling with the diagnosis; it was understanding that changes were being made for me in areas like school, my social life, and within my family. These weren't changes I chose, but ones that the circumstances dictated. The following sections will explore some of the life changes that followed my diagnosis. I aim to provide guidance on how a diagnosis can transform your life, inspiring others to anticipate these changes and find the necessary support or mental health resources to navigate them with greater ease.

School & Graduation

Following my MS diagnosis, my high school experience was turned upside down. Almost immediately, I found myself in and out of the hospital, and as a result, I never returned to the traditional high school setting. My life, once busy with typical school events and activities, was now navigating through a maze of medical challenges and adjustments.

In actuality, returning to high school became the least of my concerns. My family and I were in survival mode, trying to manage the daily realities of living with MS. The symptoms I experienced, such as optic neuritis causing blurriness in my eyes, ataxia making movement difficult, and a constant heavy feeling in my legs, disrupted every aspect of my daily life. My memory was affected, making school an impossibility. Simple tasks like getting dressed or brushing my teeth required my parents' assistance due to my weakness and lack of coordination.

There was an attempt to continue my education through virtual learning, hoping I could still participate in classes from home. However, this plan was short-lived due to frequent hospital stays and evolving symptoms. The decision to undergo chemotherapy in May 2004 made it clear that returning to a traditional school setting was out of the question.

Despite these challenges and my absence from school, my dedication to my studies prior to my diagnosis—taking Advanced Placement classes and extra coursework—meant that my school awarded me the opportunity to graduate with my classmates. This act of understanding and support from my school was a tremendous relief and joy, offering a glimmer of normalcy in an otherwise tumultuous time.

Due to an ongoing MS relapse at the time of my high school graduation ceremony in early summer 2004, walking was a significant challenge and the heat posed an additional concern. My mobility was limited; I could only walk short distances around the house with support due to balance issues. Despite these hurdles, my dream was to walk across the stage at my graduation.

The ceremony was set to take place outside on the track field, and thankfully, arrangements were made for our car to be on the field, allowing me to be as close to the ceremony as possible. It was crucial for me to stay cool due to my sensitivity to heat exacerbating my MS symptoms. As the graduation procession started, the song "You Raise Me Up" by Josh Groban played—a fitting anthem for what I was about to attempt. Initially, the plan was for my dad to wheel me to the stage area when my name was called. However, I had a different idea in mind—I wanted to walk with the aid of my cane.

My dad assisted me out of the car and into the wheelchair, navigating the bumpy grass to our designated spot. As my name approached, I expressed my desire to walk. My dad was hesitant but understood how important this was to me. After helping me to stand, he reluctantly let go of my arm as I steadied myself with the cane.

With every step towards the stage, my legs felt incredibly heavy and unstable. I focused intently on the teacher holding my diploma, moving forward despite not feeling the ground beneath my feet. This walk was a true testament of faith—moving forward despite challenges, trusting in God's guidance and strength. The cheers from my family and friends propelled me to keep going until I finally reached the stage and received my diploma. Exhausted but triumphant, I found relief in my dad's presence and the wheelchair waiting to take me back to the comfort of our air-conditioned car.

Reflecting on this moment, I realize the significance of my family's support. Walking at graduation was more than just a physical achievement; it symbolized overcoming the immense obstacles I faced that year. It wasn't about the aesthetics of the walk but the determination and courage it took to make it happen. This milestone was a powerful reminder of what I could accomplish with determination and the support of my loved ones.

Social Life

Returning home after my first hospital stay due to Multiple Sclerosis, I was warmly greeted by a living room transformed by my school and church friends. Balloons, cards, and stuffed animals covered the fireplace landing, among them a big yellow smiley face balloon that seemed to symbolize the hope I clung to. Initially, the visits from friends and their parents brought much-needed normalcy and laughter to my days as we chatted about TV shows and school gossip. Yet, as the weeks passed, these visits dwindled, leaving me to face the reality of my condition in solitude as my peers moved forward with their lives, preparing for college and the experiences I had dreamed of sharing with them.

Many of my friends were unaware of the full impact of MS on my life, and I wasn't ready to explain it to them. The assumption by some at my high school graduation that my wheelchair use was due to a simple injury like a broken leg showed the disconnect between my reality and their perceptions. It took quite some time for me to come to terms with the fact that my path would diverge significantly from that of my friends. While they looked forward to college and the adventures it promised, I was left to navigate the complexities of life with MS, a quest that promised its own set of challenges and lessons, far removed from the typical high school to college transition.

At 18, when friends were my world, the impact of losing them to my battle with Multiple Sclerosis was very hard. Sitting alone, looking through Myspace and Facebook in my wheelchair, the joy of their college experiences contrasted sharply with my own reality. It felt as though life had pressed fast forward for them, while I was paused, grappling with an illness that seemed to erase me from their worlds. The isolation that came with MS was as crippling as its physical manifestations. Attempts to reconnect with friends felt like bridging worlds apart—mine, defined by mobility aids and endless medical appointments, and theirs, filled with the freedoms of youth and new beginnings. Conversations with them became a mirror reflecting the divergence of our paths; they shared tales of campus life and love, while I could only offer insights into the awful types of hospital food I had endured and the changing reflection in the mirror. Despite the steadfast support of my family, the absence of those friendships at a time when such bonds are everything left a void no amount of familial love could fill. The longing for understanding, for friends who would weather the storm of MS alongside me, became a not so silent plea. This period underscored a harsh truth: chronic illness doesn't just steal your health; it can dim the light of friendships that once seemed unshakeable, leaving you adrift in a sea of isolation at a time when you need those anchors the most.

Navigating the complexities of friendships after my diagnosis was incredibly challenging. There were rare occasions when friends from college would visit, but by then, everything about me had changed dramatically—I could hardly participate in activities the way they could. My appearance and abilities had evolved significantly due to my condition.

During a college break, a friend invited me to my very first party. Despite my excitement, my illness made me apprehensive about attending. My concern was twofold: I feared being judged for my changed appearance I had gained an incredible amount of weight in a short period of time due to medications and for needing a cane to walk. In an attempt to blend in, I made a significant decision to leave my cane in the car upon arriving at the party, a choice driven by my desire to not appear different.

This decision led to an embarrassing incident. As we approached the party's entrance, I tripped on the curb and fell face-first onto the ground. Although my hands managed to break my fall somewhat, the embarrassment was overwhelming. I felt a deep sense of humiliation, not just for myself but also for putting my friend in an awkward position by inviting me. Inside the party, a few guests inquired if I was alright, which only added to my embarrassment. This incident reminded me of my reliance on the cane for balance, highlighting the differences that made me feel so out of place.

Feeling out of place with my peers started to become a familiar sensation for me. On another occasion, when I was about 19 or 20 years old, some high school friends returned home for a college break. They shared stories of their college experiences and adventures, which was thrilling to hear. Then, they invited me to join them for a day out at the mall that weekend, marking the first time since high school that friends had included me in their plans. Despite my excitement, I was apprehensive about their reaction to my changed appearance.

My treatment regimen, which included chemotherapy and steroids, had significantly altered my appearance. From a slender 130 pounds at 5'8" in high school, my weight had significantly increased to 200 pounds a year later. Additionally, the steroids caused "moon face," a condition where my face became puffy and round. These changes were undeniable every time I looked in the mirror.

That weekend, my friend picked me up for a long-awaited trip to the mall. I had carefully prepared for the day, making sure to bring my cell phone and my cane, which had become a necessary tool for balance after my recent hospital stay. Despite the cane's discreet design, its presence was a constant reminder of my condition. Our car ride to the mall was filled with lighthearted chatter about music, boys, and old school memories, reigniting the camaraderie we shared.

The excitement of meeting a friend's college boyfriend and his friends at the mall was dampened when, upon parking, my friend suggested I leave my cane behind to avoid drawing attention. Torn between wanting to fit in and knowing my limitations, I faced a dilemma. The risk of navigating the crowded mall without my cane was too high, considering my recent hospitalization and the tripping accident I had at the party a year or so before.

After a moment of hesitation, I chose safety over appearances, explaining the necessity of the cane to avoid tripping. Despite a brief look of skepticism from my friend, we proceeded into the mall, me with my cane in hand. The day unfolded with new introductions and casual shopping. I couldn't shake off a sense of being slightly out of place.

The day ended with a polite drop-off at my home, leaving me with mixed feelings of gratitude for the outing and embarrassment over my dependence on the cane. Unfortunately, this would be the last time I spent with those friends from high school. It wasn't just the cane that distanced us; our lives were heading in different directions. They went back to college, while I faced another MS relapse and hospital stay shortly after. Our paths, which had once converged during school days, had now diverged, reflecting the changing dynamics of friendships and life's unpredictable course.

For the first few years, my illness led to a significant degree of isolation. The uncertainty of how to interact with someone who's visibly or functionally changed creates a barrier not just for friends and acquaintances, but also for oneself. The physical and emotional changes that come with an illness can make the idea of venturing out less appealing, fostering a preference for solitude over facing the outside world. Additionally, there's a pervasive fear of becoming a burden on others, which can further discourage attempts to engage socially or ask for help when needed.

A conversation I once had highlights this isolation vividly. Someone mentioned never seeing individuals in wheelchairs while out shopping or on their daily errands. My response was straightforward; navigating public spaces can be daunting. The challenge isn't just about dealing with judgmental stares or comments but practical issues like inadequate accessibility or difficult parking contribute to the reluctance. Moreover, the anxiety over imposing on others or requiring assistance for tasks that were once simple exacerbates the situation. These barriers, both social and physical, often limit our engagement with the world around us, making the effort seem insurmountable at times.

Family Life

Lastly, my family's support and encouragement were never more evident than when I was diagnosed with MS at age 18. I cannot adequately express how life-changing my diagnosis and disability were for my parents and siblings. During my illness, my parents had to make significant changes to their lives and hard decisions for our family and I. The care team at Johns Hopkins Hospital in Baltimore detailed the aggressiveness of the MS. The Johns Hopkins specialists had never seen anything like my MRI images before in someone so young, and particularly not an African American female. There were lesions throughout my brain and spinal cord. My parents watched the life-altering effects MS was having on me, including repeated loss of function in my legs. They faced the difficult decision of whether to pursue chemotherapy, even if it meant risking my infertility in the future. Their first priority was my health so that I could have a future. My mom was adamant I would survive.

Unfortunately, my parents frustratingly encountered many practitioners who put their hands up in confusion and defeat. The medical experts told us at several points over the years this was as good as it could get for me. They told us I would not be able to walk on my own 10 years after my diagnosis without the assistance of a walker or cane. I could possibly be confined to a wheelchair. I am sure that continually receiving such news had a profound, overwhelming effect on my mom and dad. But Mom and Dad never faltered in their advocacy for me and my health, and insisted and expected excellence of care. My father was my rock, my support, my prayer intercessor, and the one who always believed there was more in store for me than the doctors predicted. My mom made it a point to speak personally to each doctor to see what we could do to manage the MS and improve my mobility. She stayed many times with me in the hospital overnight. She even went through the arduous task of ensuring my enrollment in Medicare at such a young age to have adequate insurance coverage. Oddly enough, I was eligible to get Medicare because I had been an I-CARE Inc. employee since the age of 14 and had paid into the system. Mom did not know that incorporating me into the family business at such a young age would impact my future as much as it did. She also applied for incapacitation determination, which allowed me to be on my parents' insurance plan indefinitely due to my chronic "progressive" disease. Having Medicare as primary coverage, and their commercial insurance as secondary, I was able to get all my treatments and hospital stays covered. This absolutely was a benefit to my health.

During this challenging period, my mom was an incredible source of support and advocacy. She attended every doctor's visit with me, asking pertinent questions and ensuring we both understood my treatment plans. She was vigilant during my hospital stays, making sure I had everything I needed, and that the hospital staff provided the proper care. Whether it was a routine hospitalization or an unexpected visit to the emergency room, she was always by my side, offering comfort and hope.

Her support went beyond just being there physically; she shared in my emotional trips through highs and lows, praying with me and sharing tears during the tough times. Having her hand in mine was a constant reminder of her commitment. Crucially, she acted as my voice, advocating for me when I couldn't speak for myself. Her relentless efforts to ensure I received the best care and her steadfast support made facing my condition a bit more manageable, always reminding me that I wasn't going through this alone.

My dad treated our time together in the hospital as special, though it was not where we would have preferred to be. Once in a while he would sneak me into the hospital cafeteria and buy me treats to keep me in good spirits. When I was discharged from the hospital, my dad would drive out of the parking lot with screeching tires, as if we were escaping. Dad would always repeat his refrain. "Ash, next year is going to be better. I promise you, next year is going to be better." This is someone who watched me repeatedly lose use of my functions. Even when I couldn't use my legs or see out of one eye, my dad's words helped me fight to get better. He drew from his strong faith, that God would always provide for us, and that He loved and cared for His children. And I believed my dad. He was right; each year there were improvements. His inspiration to see a glimmer of hope in a seemingly hopeless situation was priceless to me and my recovery.

My fondest memories in the hospital are of playing spades with my dad. I remember him going to the gift shop and buying playing cards. We even adjusted the game and called it two-handed spades. The cards were dealt, and the players picked from one pile. Each player did not know what was in the other's hand. We played it repeatedly and for hours. It was something just for us. Playing spades was not just about the game; it was about the time spent with my dad. We still play our game to this day. It always makes me happy. My dad was an incredible encouragement me when I was in the hospital. He insisted on staying overnight when he could. If I had a private room, he would sleep on the small cot next to my bed. Dad would ask my care providers to explain medical procedures or information in a way I could understand. He would cry and pray for me. He would do his best to make jokes and make me laugh. One time, the medication I was given affected my vision. When I looked at my dad, I saw two heads. I thought it was hilarious. It then became our inside joke: "Dad, you have two heads!"

Aside from the frequent hospital stays, my parents had to make innumerable changes to their lives. They sacrificed many commitments and activities they would normally enjoy, such as date nights, vacations and time at church. My parents did whatever they could to make life easier for me while I was dealing with the MS relapses. Upon the doctors' predictions of continued loss of mobility, my dad used his engineering expertise to modify our home to be more accommodating. He converted our living room into a bedroom for me and added doors on either side of it. He installed ramps and a stair lift, ensuring I had as much access as possible to our home. He made sure our home still felt like home to me. The changes allowed me to safely navigate around the house. Now, my dad does home modification management for individuals and families when a loved one experiences changes in mobility. His team installs grab bars, stair lifts, widens doors, and does bathroom and kitchen remodels. This ensures the person with differing abilities feels safe in their home. My dad's motto is, "We'll modify your home, so you don't have to modify your life." I love my parents. They were prepared for the worst but hoped and prayed for the best.

The realization of how deeply my MS diagnosis affected my siblings didn't hit me until much later. Being the eldest, I had always been the leader, the trailblazer for my younger sister and brother. I was the one who would confidently stride forward, introducing us to new acquaintances and rekindling connections with those we hadn't seen in a while. My siblings, more reserved by nature, would find comfort in my shadow, knowing I was there to pave the way.

However, MS shifted this dynamic drastically. I could no longer be that guiding force. Suddenly, I became the focal point of our family's concern, drawing our parents' attention away from my siblings due to the endless doctor's appointments and hospital stays. It pains me to think about the impact this had on them. Our family outings, the events we used to enjoy together, were all but forgotten in the wake of my illness. When you are the one battling a disease, it's challenging to see the ripples it sends through the lives of those around you. My sister and brother, as they confided in me later, felt they had lost their parents to my illness, and I still carry the weight of that revelation.

The changes in our family's dynamics were stark and immediate. I remember a poignant moment when my sister, at 16, needed to take her driving test. My father, who would have traditionally been by her side, was with me in the hospital. Instead, a kind member of our church stepped in to take her. Our church community became an extended family, filling in gaps where my parents couldn't, due to their commitment to my care. Though their support was invaluable, it couldn't replace the presence of our parents during critical moments in my siblings' lives. The mental toll on my siblings was profound, a realization I fully grasped only after becoming a parent myself. When my son was six weeks old there was an accident at our home, I feared had injured him. I was so consumed with fear and worry for him that everything else blurred into the background, including my daughter. The ambulance arrived, and in my panic, I unintentionally ignored her needs. Thankfully, my son was fine, but that episode left a lasting impression on me about how easily one child's crisis can eclipse the needs of another.

When my little brother graduated high school, he did a graduation speech at our church that really brought this home. He shared how his entry into high school coincided with the onset of my illness, reshaping his teenage years. His experiences were tinged with responsibilities and concerns far beyond what most of his peers faced.

Looking back, I realize the importance of comprehensive family support in times of illness. Counseling for each family member, both individually and as a group, is crucial. It's a way to ensure that while the family navigates the challenges of the illness together, each person's individual experience and emotional well-being are also addressed. I know now that my parents did the best they could under the circumstances, but I wish we had all understood sooner the far-reaching effects of my MS on the whole family. The journey of living with a chronic illness is a shared one, with each person's path intertwined yet distinct.

Conclusion

Over many years, I embarked on an exploration of self-discovery to identify and grasp the reality of the diagnosis and my emotions around it. Despite the challenges of living with a life-altering disease, my faith refused to let my mind succumb to the prognosis I was given. There is no known cure for Multiple Sclerosis (MS). I was told it was progressive, therefore, the disease and symptoms would get worse over time and could lead to permanent disability. For many years I experienced relapses when the disease was extremely active, and then remissions when the disease was quiet. I found out over time that this back-and-forth of quick, intense debilitation, followed by miraculous recovery, was challenging for me physically, mentally, and emotionally.

Reflecting on those tumultuous years, I recall the emotional rollercoaster that accompanied the physical one. The highs of feeling 'normal', where MS seemed like a distant memory, were exciting and welcomed. However, these were invariably followed by devastating lows of an MS relapse, where I was left incapacitated, reliant on others for the most basic of tasks. The frequency and intensity of these cycles in the early stages of my disease left me angry and resentful. There were so many times where I felt like it just "wasn't fair". I felt trapped in a body that had totally betrayed me, subject to the whims of an unpredictable disease.

Over time, and with much introspection and prayer, my perspective shifted. I learned to transform resentment into gratitude. Gratitude for the periods of remission, however brief, where I could have fun and do things on my own. Gratitude for the strength I didn't know I had, which emerged through each battle with a relapse. I also learned to turn my anger into perseverance. This perseverance was essential to my recovery from relapses where I had to learn how to walk and use my hands again. In my twenties, the cycles of devastating relapses and miraculous remissions shaped me, challenging me emotionally in ways I never anticipated. The experience has taught me that life with MS isn't about waiting for the storm to pass; it's about learning to dance in the rain.

Chapter 7

My Secret Sauce

This 20-year MS odyssey has been filled with highs and lows, trials and triumphs. I've faced countless treatments and medications and read tons of books and articles in pursuit of my path toward wellness. Reflecting on these two decades, I'm filled with gratefulness because, against all odds and despite the poor prognosis that once loomed over me, I've been blessed to avoid any permanent disability. It's not the result of a single miraculous remedy, a secret treatment unveiled, or a groundbreaking medication. Instead, it's about a blend of elements, a 'secret sauce' that has been curated over the years.

If you're curious about how I've reached this point despite the hurdles that "were" and "are," let me share my recipe. I've always had a passion for cooking and finding joy and peace in the kitchen. The most memorable sauces I've whipped up—those that leave people asking for more—are often the ones made from the simplest ingredients. Yet, it's the process of blending these ingredients, letting them simmer together, and allowing them to sit and meld their flavors overnight in the refrigerator that transforms them into something extraordinary. The sauce somehow becomes richer, deeper, and more flavorful, demonstrating the brilliance of time and simplicity.

Consider the following chapters as the ingredients of my secret sauce, a compilation of simple yet powerful elements that have intermingled and marinated over two decades. These ingredients have been the cornerstone of my successful management of this disease. It's important to note that what I'm sharing isn't a medical prescription or a replacement for professional advice. My story doesn't come with the guarantee of replicating my experience but rather offers insight into the strategies that have helped me navigate the road to peace with this disease.

So, I invite you to read on if you're interested in discovering the blend of lifestyle choices, mindset shifts, and personal philosophies that have been my allies in this long battle. This narrative doesn't just chronicle my struggle; it's a testament to resilience, adaptability, and the power of combining simple, everyday 'ingredients' to create a life that, despite its challenges, is fulfilling and rich. Welcome to the unveiling of my secret sauce, a mix that has simmered for over 20 years and that has guided me to remarkable success, both mentally and physically, living with Multiple Sclerosis.

Chapter 8

Secret Sauce #1

Positive Mindset: How Thoughts Transform Experiences

Living with the ups and downs of Multiple Sclerosis (MS) has been a profound learning experience about myself, especially how I respond to pressure and what truly motivates me. I discovered an intriguing aspect of my motivation: tell me I can't do something, and I'll use that doubt as fuel to prove you wrong. It's as if there's a "motivation button" on my chest, ready to be pressed whenever I'm faced with comments like I won't be able to walk again, "This is your new normal," or doubts that I would regain my use of my right hand. Hitting that imaginary "motivator" button has always spurred me into action, helping me accomplish what was deemed impossible.

While I've often joked about this imaginary motivator button on my chest, I'm aware the real power lies in my mind. It's my mindset that transforms challenges into achievable goals. Believing that obstacles can be overcome has made tackling them far more manageable. As I've grown and continued this journey with MS, I've realized that relying solely on external skepticism for motivation is limiting and unsustainable. What if the doubts stop coming? Will my drive to succeed diminish? It has taught me the importance of finding motivation from within, recognizing that the strongest push comes from my inner resolve and determination to thrive, regardless of the external voices.

I've found that the key to facing Multiple Sclerosis, and indeed any challenge in my life, was to dig deep and find that inner drive. It meant reshaping my thoughts and altering how I viewed each obstacle. I had to pump myself up, finding my own drive from within. Motivation that originates internally requires a shift in thinking, altering my perspective of the challenge. Motivation and a changed perspective turned my obstacles into stepping stones for perseverance and personal growth, not only in managing the MS but in every aspect of my life.

This change in perspective transformed my entire approach—how I manage my health, overcome difficult days, and stay motivated. It's astonishing how significantly our thoughts can influence our bodies. Believing something will be bad almost guarantees it will be. Yet, choosing to adopt a positive mindset alters how I perceive and react to situations. Even if the external circumstances remain constant for a time, a positive approach not only makes the experience more bearable but can eventually bring about real changes in those circumstances. For me, keeping a positive outlook is essential.

A few months back, as I was driving home, the skies suddenly opened, and rain began to pour down in sheets. Almost instantly, the roads clogged up, and there I was, trapped in my car, surrounded by a relentless downpour and the creeping pace of traffic. At that moment, I stood at a crossroads in my mind. I could either stare out at the rain, cursing its timing and letting fear creep in with thoughts of potential accidents, or I could choose a different path. I decided to turn on my favorite podcast, filling the space around me with words of inspiration and calm. As the sound of rain drumming against the car blended with the uplifting dialogue, my car transformed. No longer was it a cage of frustration in a storm; it became a quiet corner of the world where I could recharge, lost in thought and motivation. Outside, the rain continued to fall, unchanged and unyielding, yet how I experienced that moment shifted entirely. The traffic and the rain, once sources of stress, became the backdrop to a period of reflection and inner peace. This choice didn't stop the rain or clear the roads, but it altered my reality within those circumstances, demonstrating how a change in mindset can profoundly affect our experience, and in doing so, transform our circumstances from hindrances into opportunities.

Many people advocate for the "fake it 'till you make it" philosophy, but that never resonated with me. I live by "make it 'till you make it." This slight tweak in wording signifies a profound shift. It means not even entertaining the thought of pretense, recognizing that authenticity is something your body can sense. By committing to making, I've refused to consider failure as a possibility, which has not only helped me navigate my MS but also made it mentally more bearable. Adopting this mindset transforms the experience from one of constant disappointment and bitterness into a lesson in resilience and finding strength. Viewing every piece of "bad news" or challenge not as a definitive setback but as an opportunity to bolster my perseverance gives me a sense of control in situations that might otherwise feel overwhelming. This mental shift empowers me, ensuring that even if my physical circumstances remain the same, my perception and happiness don't have to. That sense of inner peace and power is something no one can take from me. It's about finding calm in the chaos, a lesson in inner strength that has been invaluable in my life.

When my main neurologist first told me, "This is a good time to have MS," I was taken aback. His words seemed bizarre, especially right after he had outlined what Multiple Sclerosis entails and its long-term implications. However, as I learned more, I began to understand his perspective. At the time of my diagnosis, the medical field was seeing a surge in new, effective treatments for MS, with even more promising options on the horizon. These advancements were changing the game for how MS was managed. Additionally, being diagnosed at a young age was described as an advantage. Doctors suggested that my youth was beneficial, likely implying physical resilience, but I discovered another layer of this advantage: mindset. Unlike some older individuals who might resign themselves to their fate upon receiving a diagnosis, thinking they've lived a full life, my youth meant I had everything to live for. At 18, I was just starting out, and the idea of giving up wasn't an option.

This mindset wasn't a denial of my condition but a commitment to continually strive for better, without setting limits on the effort. "Until" became my guiding principle, an open-ended commitment to keep going, without specifying what the end might look like. This perspective, fostered in the face of youth and the drive to experience life, taught me an invaluable lesson: my experience with MS—or any significant challenge—is about relentless pursuit, not resignation. Rooted in the urgency and optimism of youth, this approach can be a powerful mindset for anyone, at any age. It's about living with the conviction that there's always more to strive for, more life to live, and those obstacles, no matter how daunting, won't create limits or define our attitude.

My positive attitude comes from a heart of gratitude. What really makes me smile is waking up with thankfulness in my heart for everything I do have, instead of focusing on what I don't have. I do not take anything for granted. Leaning into joy and smiling even when it is difficult has helped me to reduce my stress. Positivity is healing for me. It is how I de-stress in a world that wants to give us stress all the time. I have used it during sickness, and it has made a difference in my recovery. I know the physical benefits of something as simple as a smile. We feel better, even if for a moment, when our brains release dopamine upon smiling. I recall one nurse who came to my home weekly, and she influenced my day with her positive attitude and smile. It was essential for me to hear her say she would help me through it. It helped me change my own attitude, too.

It has taken me nearly 20 years, but after much progress I can say I am grateful for this challenge of MS. And by grateful, I mean I see purpose in my pain. It has taught me invaluable lessons. It has pushed me to give excellent care to my patients. It allows me to be compassionate to their pain and struggles. I am glad that I wasn't in charge of my life plan; God was. He knew the road I was destined to take. He needed to take me on so I would be able to understand and help serve others.

Chapter 9

Secret Sauce #2
Embracing Vitality: Harnessing Fitness and Nutrition in MS Care

For me, living with Multiple Sclerosis (MS) is not just a battle against symptoms and flare-ups; it's a continuous quest to maintain and enhance my quality of life through thoughtful self-care. It has taught me the invaluable role of physical activity and dietary choices that fuel my ability to stay active. Each day presents an opportunity to engage in exercise and choose nourishment that helps me maintain and enhance my mobility with MS. This realization became even more profound as I discovered the mental health benefits of regular exercise. The dopamine release, often referred to as the "happy chemical," during physical activity, played a significant role in boosting my mood and motivation. This aspect of fitness helped combat some of the challenging moments I faced with MS, providing a mental resilience that complemented the physical efforts. Yes, fitness was about exercising my body and maintaining movement, but equally important it was about enriching my mind, keeping me motivated and happier. This has been a key part of my strategy to live well with MS and has been pivotal in my self-care regimen. This chapter delves into how I learned the benefits of adopting a consistent, but easy, fitness regimen and eating foods that facilitated this movement.

Movement: The Foundation of Recovery

During times of an MS relapse, my mobility was significantly compromised, turning every attempt at movement into an uphill battle. It felt like I was in a personal fight against gravity itself. There were moments when simply moving an arm or leg felt like an insurmountable task challenged by the invisible chains of immobility MS imposed. Mentally, it was equally challenging; instructing a limb to move without any response highlighted the frustrations with managing this condition. It appeared that movement and MS were in direct conflict, with the disease striving to halt my movement but movement being crucial in regaining my abilities during a flare-up. During these times I embraced the principle of Newton's first law of motion as inspiration. I understood that a body at rest tends to stay at rest, and a body in motion tends to stay in motion. This principle proved true during the challenging times I faced with MS and mobility. Despite the disease's efforts to restrict movement, I discovered that embracing motion, no matter how minimal, becomes a critical countermeasure to the disease's constraints. My own experiences have shown that movement and MS can indeed coexist, with physical activity serving as an invaluable ally in the battle for mobility and independence.

Getting back into exercise after a relapse was challenging, but I recognized the need to create my own momentum and push forward. I distinctly remember a time after recovering from a relapse when I was committed to resuming my treadmill workouts. I started my treadmill regimen with modest expectations, setting the machine to its lowest speed and no incline, aiming for just five minutes. Those initial five minutes proved to be a significant challenge, leaving me exhausted, sweaty, and clinging to the handrails for support. Yet, the sense of achievement I felt afterwards was undeniable. I didn't let myself quit before reaching that five-minute mark. Determined, I continued this routine daily, repeating the five-minute sessions for weeks until they became less strenuous, and I no longer needed to hold onto the treadmill for balance.

During these sessions, I discovered the power of positive self-talk. Encouraging myself with phrases like "I love doing this!", "Walking on the treadmill is my favorite part of the day,". "This is so much fun!" helped make the task more enjoyable. Even though it sounded a bit silly, this mental strategy worked wonders, making me eager for my next session.

Gradually, I increased my time on the treadmill. From mastering five minutes, I moved to six, then seven and a half, carefully advancing as each became more manageable. Within three months, I could walk for an hour without difficulty. This progression wasn't just about physical endurance; it was mental too. Each step forward was a boost to my confidence and determination. This experience highlighted the close connection between physical and mental health, showing me that being active benefits not just physical symptom management but also mental wellness.

Embracing a gradual and positive approach to exercise with MS was transformative, both physically and mentally. The natural dopamine boost from exercise was not just a physical uplift but also a crucial mental health support, helping me navigate the emotional challenges of the condition. This highlighted the deep connection between physical activity and mental wellness, underlining the dual benefits of exercise in managing MS symptoms and fostering a positive mental state.

My experience has shown me that with patience and a step-by-step approach, the barriers posed by MS can be surmounted. It illustrated the value of setting realistic goals and the effectiveness of positive self-talk in making exercise a sustainable part of my daily life. From the start, the need to stay active was clear, especially during flare-ups when I felt most vulnerable to the temptation of staying inactive. Simple activities like ankle pumps and limb movements, though modest, were crucial in maintaining momentum and demonstrated the principle that movement is essential for managing MS.

In my professional life as a clinician, I encountered many patients who showed reluctance towards traditional forms of exercise. Recognizing the importance of adaptability, I often turned to everyday items like cans of food as impromptu weights. This approach not only demonstrated the accessibility of physical activity but also highlighted the effectiveness of integrating movement into daily routines, however unconventional they might seem.

Five Personal Strategies for Staying Active

#1 Start Small

In my darkest moments, when MS seemed to claim victory over my body, I found solace and progress in the smallest movements. Simple ankle pumps or gently mobilizing my limbs in bed laid the groundwork for recovery during relapses.

#2 Incorporate Movement into Daily Routines

Utilizing everyday items like cans of vegetables as makeshift weights demonstrated that effective exercise doesn't require elaborate equipment. This approach not only facilitated physical engagement but also seamlessly integrated activity into my routine, proving that movement could be both accessible and enjoyable.

#3 Set Incremental Goals

My return to the gym post-relapse was marked by setting modest, achievable targets. Beginning with just five minutes on the treadmill and gradually increasing the duration instilled in me a sense of progress and accomplishment, reinforcing the importance of persistence and gradual improvement.

#4 Embrace the Power of Positivity

Speaking affirmations and positive self-talk became a mantra that propelled me forward. Convincing myself of the joy and benefits of exercise transformed my mindset, making each session on the treadmill not just a physical activity but a celebration of capability and progress.

#5 Maintain Consistency

My commitment to walking 30 minutes every weekday morning is a testament to the value of consistency. This ritual, more than just exercise, is a moment of gratitude and reflection, a daily reminder of how far I've come and the incredible journey still ahead.

Nutrition: The Foundation of Wellness

First off, let me be clear: no diet has been scientifically proven to cure Multiple Sclerosis (MS). When I received my diagnosis, well-intentioned friends flooded me with books claiming miracle diets could cure MS or even reverse its debilitating effects. After experimenting with everything from unrestricted diets to those strictly free from gluten, sugar, carbs, etc., I can assert that no specific diet has seemed to change the course of MS for me directly. I had MS relapses and remissions regardless of my diet. However, it's unmistakably clear that my dietary choices have a profound impact on both my physical mobility and mental functionality.

My personal journey has shown me that consuming foods high in sugar, processed ingredients, and fats while skimping on whole foods made me feel mentally sluggish and physically constrained. On the flip side, focusing on whole foods noticeably enhanced my mental clarity and improved my ability to move. The weight gain associated with medications like steroids only highlighted the vital role of nutrition even more. Gaining weight hindered my mobility, which was the last thing I wanted as I navigated MS and its quest to limit my movement.

By sharing my experience, I hope to inspire others to consider "mobility eating"—choosing foods that energize you and facilitate movement—as a crucial part of their health and wellness routine.

In the first year after being diagnosed with Multiple Sclerosis (MS), I gained over 80 pounds, a significant increase that was largely influenced by the high-dose steroids and other medications prescribed to me. These treatments heightened my sense of hunger, while the MS relapses reduced my physical activity. During this challenging period, my parents, who needed support, received an outpouring of kindness from friends and our church community, who regularly delivered homemade meals. Our fridge was always filled with a variety of lovingly prepared dishes. However, the steroids had another side effect, insomnia. This meant I was often awake—and hungry—at all hours of the night, a troublesome duo.

Frequent hospital stays for MS relapses meant I became a familiar face to many of the hospital staff, including the cafeteria workers. They often provided me with large, indulgent breakfasts rich in oil, butter, and sugar. While these meals were tasty, they weren't what my body needed. My eating habits were less about physical hunger and more about seeking comfort. Battling loneliness and frustration over my physical limitations made food a significant emotional crutch for me. This experience highlighted the complex relationship between diet and not just physical health, but emotional well-being, underscoring how profoundly what I eat can impact both my body's and brain's functionality.

During a hospital stay for an MS relapse that affected both my leg function and arm mobility, I was engaged in daily physical therapy sessions. These were aimed at restoring arm movement. At the same time, I was taking medication to reduce the inflammation caused by the MS relapse, so I could regain movement. One morning, my doctor caught sight of my lavish hospital breakfast and, without much commentary, covered my plate with the tray lid, looked me straight in the eyes, and stated firmly, "Ashley, you don't need to eat that." His blunt intervention shocked me, prompting a moment of reflection about my food choices. This incident served as a crucial wake-up call, illuminating the fact that I had been overlooking the significant impact what I ate had on my mobility. I was in the hospital trying to regain my mobility, but eating foods that made it hard for me to move. It really highlighted that managing MS wasn't only about fighting the disease to stay mobile but also dealing with weight gain, which further limited my movement. The weight gain was driven by emotional eating, medication side effects, and the limited physical activity that comes with MS.

If you're curious about what I eat now and what has worked for me in managing my life with this disease, my answer is simple: I eat whatever keeps me moving. I love food and see it as fuel, but I avoid anything that makes me feel sluggish or overly tired. I gravitate towards foods that energize me. Personally, I'm drawn to eating a rainbow of fruits and vegetables to ensure I get a wide range of nutrients. There was a time when I explored a completely plant-based diet, which was an exciting challenge. It pushed me to discover new plant varieties, each bursting with different colors and unique flavors, making my meals not only nutritious but also visually appealing and delicious.

This experience taught me the importance of a diet rich in natural fiber, which not only aids in keeping the body active but also ensures smooth internal functions. Fiber is crucial for preventing issues like constipation, allowing for a healthy digestive system which is crucial with illnesses like MS. While I do include fish, poultry, and other foods in my diet, my main criteria are that they must keep me active and not leave me feeling too full or stationary. Drinking plenty of water is also a key part of my routine, contributing to my overall mobility.

When I feel my food needs a bit more salt, I opt for adding extra seasoning instead to enhance the flavors. Often, what it really needs is a bit more oregano, thyme, rosemary, or a splash of lemon juice rather than extra salt. I've also learned to make my own salad dressings and marinades with just a few basic ingredients from my kitchen. It's satisfying to create these from scratch because I know exactly what's going on in them, and they taste significantly better. I've even started making my own spice blends. I use a dehydrator to dry out certain vegetables, crush them, and then sprinkle them as seasoning on my dishes. It's a fantastic way to boost flavor naturally.

So, when people ask me what I eat, I tell them I choose foods that keep me moving and living my best life. Emphasizing colorful fruits and vegetables and ensuring proper hydration have been key to keeping my energy up and maintaining mobility.

Key Insights on Mindful Eating When on Medications

Be Prepared for Medication-Induced Hunger

If you're aware that your medication might ramp up your appetite, strategize ahead of time. Focus on meal prepping with a priority on fresh vegetables. Stock up on wholesome snacks like celery with hummus or strawberries with cucumbers. This way, when hunger strikes, you're reaching for nutritious whole foods that not only satisfy but also nourish your body.

Understanding Emotional vs. Physical Hunger

Understanding the difference between eating to fill an emotional void and eating for actual nutritional needs is crucial. If you find yourself reaching for food as a source of comfort rather than out of hunger, it might be time to explore other avenues of fulfillment. Seeking counseling can be a powerful step towards understanding and managing emotional eating. Additionally, diversifying your interests and finding hobbies that engage you in non-food-related activities can provide a more sustainable source of satisfaction and happiness. This approach not only helps in addressing emotional eating but also enriches your life with varied experiences and joys beyond the kitchen.

The Role of Whole Foods

Embracing a diet rich in colorful fruits and vegetables became a cornerstone of my strategy to maintain vitality. The vibrancy of whole foods not only delighted the palate but provided the essential nutrients needed to support physical activity and overall health.

Experimentation and Flexibility

Venturing into plant-based eating expanded my culinary horizons, inviting creativity and discovery into my diet. This period of exploration taught me the importance of flexibility in dietary choices, reaffirming that the best diet is one that supports activity and energy. Go into the produce area of the grocery store and just start picking new fruits and vegetables you have never eaten before. Use online resources to learn creative ways to use that new food item.

Hydration

The simple act of drinking plenty of water emerged as a non-negotiable aspect of my daily routine. Hydration supports every facet of health, from facilitating movement to enhancing cognitive function.

Listening to My Body

Ultimately, the guiding principle of my dietary philosophy is attentiveness to my body's responses. Foods that energize and enable activity are prioritized, ensuring my diet reflects my commitment to living fully and moving freely.

The Synergy of Movement and Nutrition

The interplay between physical activity and nutrition in the context of MS care is profound. I've learned through my own experiences that keeping up with both fitness and good nutrition can make a big difference in handling MS. It's all about making smart, daily choices that fit what your body needs and what it can handle. These decisions are more than just about managing symptoms; they play a huge role in improving your overall quality of life and shaping your future. In simpler terms, finding the right balance between moving your body and fueling it with the right foods isn't just about dealing with MS—it's about thriving despite it. By focusing on both these areas, we can keep our bodies in better shape, and find joy and fulfillment along the way.

Chapter 10

Secret Sauce #3

Treatment: Navigating the Maze of Healing

Over the past twenty years, my approach to managing my health has evolved into a comprehensive strategy that extends well beyond just medications. This experience taught me the importance of being an active participant in my healthcare, particularly in enhancing my mental health and overall happiness. Recognizing that mental stress can trigger MS relapses and exacerbate the illness. I discovered the importance of engaging in activities that alleviate stress. I found that mental stress could be as taxing as physical exertion, but hobbies offered a respite, allowing me to divert my focus from my illness and find joy, regardless of whether I was at home or in the hospital. Setting life goals, such as graduating from college or achieving personal milestones like walking independently, gave me something to look forward to, fueling my excitement and desire to achieve these objectives. I found that mental stress could be as taxing as physical exertion, but hobbies offered a respite, allowing me to divert my focus from my illness and find joy, regardless of whether I was at home or in the hospital. Serving others also became a crucial part of my recovery, as it not only strengthened me but also offered profound healing benefits. This insight led me to continue to pursue a career in physical therapy, where helping others heal contributed to my own well-being. Additionally, achieving the right medication balance was essential; navigating between being overmedicated and not taking medication at all taught me the value of open communication with my healthcare team to tailor my treatment plan. These elements—goal setting, hobbies, service, and medication management—combined to form a holistic treatment plan that not only addresses the physical aspects of MS but also supports my mental health and happiness. In the following paragraphs, I'll jump into how I arrived at these conclusions and how they've supported my progress toward wellness with MS.

Having A Goal

Despite Multiple Sclerosis (MS) rerouting my life from attending the University of Miami's physical therapy program, I never lost sight of my educational aspirations. At 19, while my friends headed off to college, I found myself living life in a wheelchair at home. This didn't dampen my pursuit for education; I persuaded my parents to let me start college online at Northern Virginia Community College, beginning with two English classes. This step marked my first venture into something beyond my illness, igniting excitement within me. Success in these classes spurred me to take the next leap—attending in-person classes.

When I decided to attend classes in person, I had moved beyond relying on my wheelchair for mobility. Instead, I was using a walker or cane. My days started with my dad driving me to campus, where I'd arrive with my cane ready to support me. The specific mobility aid I needed on any given day—be it a walker or cane—wasn't important to me. What truly mattered was the exhilaration of being part of the campus community, engaging with my peers, and embracing a significant shift towards greater independence. This change from taking online classes at home and relying on a wheelchair to navigating campus with a cane or walker marked an incredible leap forward and improvement in my quality of life.

My academic pursuits didn't just provide a distraction; they became a catalyst for improvement in my MS symptoms. The more I immersed myself in school, achieving goal after goal, the more I noticed a significant reduction in MS relapses, symptoms, and hospitalizations. By the time I transferred to George Mason University a year later, I was driving independently, a complete contrast to my earlier reliance on a cane or walker for mobility around campus. I don't believe this progression was coincidental. I am convinced that the improvement in my MS symptoms and the increase in my independence are direct results of having academic goals that offered hope and something to look forward to. These goals not only kept my mind engaged but also provided me with a sense of purpose and accomplishment, which, I believe, played a key role in my physical improvements.

The transformation continued when I enrolled in the Physical Therapist Assistant program at the Medical Education Campus of Virginia, where my life's adventure came full circle. By this point, I was not just another student; I was living proof that having a purpose could fundamentally alter one's trajectory, even while dealing with a chronic illness. Having goals gave me something other than my condition to focus on, reducing the mental and physical limitations imposed by MS.

Graduating with honors in 2010 was more than an academic achievement; it was a milestone that reflected the profound impact of setting goals and pursuing dreams on managing my MS. This has taught me the invaluable lesson that having something to strive for can not only provide hope and excitement but also significantly alter the course of living with a chronic illness, transforming limitations into milestones.

Focusing on something beyond my illness became a crucial escape. Living with a chronic condition, it's all too easy to become consumed by it. When your hands or legs don't function properly, those challenges are a constant reminder—they're always with you, visible to others, and impossible to ignore. The mental burden of constantly dwelling on these issues can be as restrictive as the physical limitations themselves, affecting both mind and body. However, setting a goal like pursuing education allowed me to redirect my focus. Engaging in academic pursuits not only distracted me from my condition but also seemed to improve my symptoms. The more I immersed myself in school, the less my MS defined my daily life. Having that alternative focus—schoolwork, goals, a future—lifted some of the weight of the disease, allowing me to concentrate on something productive and fulfilling.

Finding A Hobby

Introducing a hobby into your life can truly be a game-changer. For me, cooking and gardening have been more than just pastimes – they've been lifelines. When I'm in the kitchen, experimenting with recipes and adding my own twist to dishes, I feel a sense of joy and fulfillment like nothing else. There's something incredibly therapeutic about tending to my garden, watching plants grow and thrive under my care. These hobbies have provided me with a much-needed escape from the challenges of living with MS. They remind me to appreciate the simple pleasures in life and to focus on the present moment. To bring more joy and fulfillment into your life, I highly recommend finding a hobby that speaks to your soul. Trust me, it will make all the difference.

Cooking

Cooking has become a passion of mine, and I've been told I have quite the knack for it—a skill I certainly didn't possess in my early 20s. Back then, my culinary experiments were so disastrous that my dad humorously suggested I might need to invest more in groceries. My fascination with cooking began with watching shows on the Cooking Channel and exploring various recipes. However, sticking strictly to a recipe was never my style; I preferred adding my personal twist to every dish. This creative process offered me a much-needed distraction from my MS, engaging my hands and legs in a rewarding and imaginative activity.

What I adore most about cooking is the joy it brings to others. There's a unique satisfaction in preparing a meal and witnessing the last bite enjoyed by someone else, even if it means I'm the last to eat. The act of combining simple ingredients to create something both delicious and nutritious, and then seeing the pleasure it brings to others, energizes and excites me. Cooking has been a significant part of my learning to live with MS, transforming my kitchen into a place of joy and therapy.

When I got my first place, stocking up my kitchen with an array of ingredients was exhilarating. Inviting friends over and cooking for them provided a delightful escape from the stresses of MS. It was a way to channel my energy positively, finding relief and happiness in the process. The greatest compliment I've ever been given is when people say they can taste the love in every bite of my cooking. That's exactly what I aim for! Cooking became more than just a hobby; it was a way to express love and creativity without the constraints of my condition.

I ventured into catering for a while, thinking it would amplify my passion. However, I soon realized that turning this love into a business detracted from the joy it brought me. The pleasure of cooking, for me, lies not in the profit but in the act of giving and sharing my culinary creations with others. I believe everyone should find a hobby that brings them such fulfillment, something they would joyfully do without any expectation of payment. Cooking is my form of art, my method of healing, and my way of contributing joy to the world around me.

Gardening

Gardening evolved into a refuge for me amidst my battle with MS, connecting me to my family's legacy of gardening while providing an immense sense of serenity and a much-needed distraction. My grandmother Ivey was known for her green thumb, and my father took great pride in our pristine lawn, a pride shared and contributed to by my siblings and me. Among various plants, morning glories captivated me the most. Planting their seeds, caring for the soil, and watering them daily became a cherished routine, bringing me happiness as I watched them ascend the side of our home.

This bond with gardening deepened when I acquired my first house in my late 20s, and embarked on creating my own garden. The act of plunging my hands in the soil, bending down, and nurturing each plant—marked a significant milestone from days when mobility was a challenge, reminding me of how far I'd come from relying on a wheelchair or cane.

Once a source of fear due to the risk of falling, the notion of the ground had changed for me. Where it had once loomed as a threatening space now presented itself as a canvas for my gratitude and creativity. The ability to garden, to willingly lower myself to the earth to tend to plants, marked not just a physical milestone, but a profound shift in perspective. No longer was I apprehensive about the prospect of being close to the ground; instead, I found joy and a sense of accomplishment in engaging with it directly. This transition from fear to familiarity showed my progress, symbolizing a reclaimed confidence and a newfound peace with my surroundings.

More than a hobby, gardening became an act of gratitude for me. It served as a poignant reminder of times when such simple pleasures were unattainable, celebrating how far I had progressed in my search for health. The thriving plants and flowers were a visible reward for my efforts, showcasing the fruits of patience, care, and a bit of sunshine.

Fundamentally, gardening was about more than just tending to plants; it was about fostering my overall health and happiness. It shifted my focus from the challenges of MS to the joys of growth and renewal. Every plant I nurtured was a small victory, a celebration of the physical and mental strength gardening provided. This pastime of cultivating my garden became a testament to life's simple pleasures, offering physical activity and serving as a constant reminder to appreciate every moment of capability and mobility.

Self-Healing Nature of Service

Helping others, surprisingly, has become a crucial part of my self-care routine. It might sound counterintuitive, but there's something deeply healing about taking the focus off yourself and extending kindness to someone else. Healing transcends medication, vital as it is. There's a different kind of remedy found in the joy of giving. I experienced this firsthand when a client, despite her own struggles, prepared peanut butter and jelly sandwiches for us, her caregivers. The act wasn't grand, but the satisfaction and sense of purpose it brought her—and the delight it brought us—was palpable. It was a clear example of how giving to others can also give back to us, boosting our spirits and mental well-being.

During tough times, like a challenging diagnosis or an unnerving treatment, it's natural to become engulfed in our own world of worries. Yet, choosing to serve others can dramatically shift our perspective, offering a glimpse of light in the darkest of times. I recall a moment in the hospital when I reached out to a friend anxious about her surgery. Praying with her not only provided her comfort but also made me realize that serving others was an integral part of my own healing. This act of kindness wasn't just for her benefit; it was a form of self-care for me, allowing me to process my emotions and find peace amidst my own turmoil.

If I could share a piece of advice with anyone facing hardships, it would be akin to a double-sided reminder: it's okay to feel angry or upset about your situation, but also consider how you can serve others. This mindset doesn't diminish the severity of our own challenges but rather offers a way to channel our experiences positively. Engaging in service is essentially self-care because it helps us to see beyond our circumstances, utilize our strengths in meaningful ways, and connect with others on a deeply human level.

Understanding that making someone else happy could also elevate my own mood has been enlightening. Service has emerged not just as an act of altruism but as a strategic component of my self-care. It has helped me manage stress, navigate my emotions, and transform my outlook on life. By focusing on what I could offer rather than what I was enduring, I discovered a profound source of healing and contentment. In essence, serving others has become a pathway to caring for myself, revealing that self-care and service are two sides of the same coin, each enriching the other in ways medication alone cannot achieve.

Treatment: Medication

From the moment I was diagnosed with MS, the aggressiveness of my condition demanded equally aggressive treatments. Doctors pointed out the numerous inflamed lesions on my brain and spinal cord, comparing my MRI images to a brightly lit Christmas tree. Within the first three months, I underwent chemotherapy and plasmapheresis to combat the intense relapses that were rapidly impairing me.

Over the years, my treatment regimen has included a wide array of approaches; intermuscular and subcutaneous shots, intravenous medications and therapies, and experimental treatments, each bringing its own set of challenges and side effects. The effectiveness of these treatments varied; some provided relief for relapses, while others had little impact. Through countless infusions and therapies, I understood the goal has always been to slow the progression of MS and minimize physical disability. However, after years of bouncing between different medications and treatments, I hit a wall in my late 20s. Feeling more like a subject in an experiment than a patient in care, the constant observation and trial of new drugs became both draining and disheartening. It was then I realized the need for a shift in direction and asked my mom to support me in taking the reins of my treatment plan. I had a doctor who seemed more interested in prescribing new medications than in understanding their effects on me. The side effects from these prescribed medications varied widely, impacting both my physical and mental state. Some days, I felt overwhelmed by fatigue, making even the simplest tasks seem insurmountable. Other times, I experienced bouts of nausea or headaches that persisted despite any attempts to alleviate them. The mental fog was perhaps the most challenging, as it clouded my thoughts and impaired my ability to focus, disconnecting me from my daily life and the people in it. Mood swings and sleep disturbances further complicated my situation, creating a cycle of stress and frustration. It became clear that the cumulative impact of these side effects was significantly diminishing my quality of life, prompting me to seek a change in my approach to treatment. The side effects from these medications piled up to the point where I found myself in a detox center. I was there getting detoxed off all the prescribed medications I was on that were given to me by my doctors to help the MS symptoms. But there I sat alongside people battling addictions to street drugs. All of us were there to cleanse our bodies. The irony of my situation was both emotionally draining and embarrassingly eye-opening. I kept asking myself, "How did I end up here?"

Leaving the detox center, I made a promise to myself to steer clear of all prescription drugs. That experience marked a significant shift in how I approached my health, leading me to seek alternatives and more holistic solutions for managing my condition.

I made a bold decision to stop all my MS medications and treatments, seeking a fresh start with holistic healthcare. I embraced a new approach, diving into understanding pain not just as a physical sensation but as a perception and exploring alternative therapies like hypnology. I revamped my diet, aiming for a healthier lifestyle, and for a while, it seemed like I had found the perfect escape from the relentless cycle of medical interventions. Life without the constant medical oversight felt liberating; I was no longer under the watchful eye of doctors waiting to respond to every new symptom with another prescription.

However, despite my initial success, I hadn't fully committed to the holistic path—I was still letting stress, my greatest trigger for MS flare-ups, dominate my life. Deep down, stress still had a tight grip on me, acting as a potent catalyst for my MS symptoms. The truth was, I struggled with letting go of worry and the tendency to fixate on problems, behaviors that only served to feed the cycle of stress. This constant state of tension was more than just an emotional burden; it had tangible, harmful effects on my body.

Stress, particularly the kind that stems from chronic worry and rumination, can significantly increase the levels of stress hormones, such as cortisol, circulating in the body. Elevated cortisol levels over prolonged periods can wreak havoc on the immune system, weakening its ability to function effectively. For someone with MS, an autoimmune disease where the body's immune system mistakenly attacks its own tissues, this imbalance can be particularly detrimental. The heightened state of alert caused by increased stress hormones exacerbates the immune system's overactivity, potentially leading to more frequent and severe flare-ups of the disease.

In my case, this meant that despite adopting healthier eating habits and exploring alternative therapies, the benefits of these changes were undermined by my inability to manage stress effectively. The preservation of these stress-inducing thought patterns not only counteracted the positive steps I was taking but also directly impacted my immune system's behavior, thus influencing the course of my MS. It became clear that to truly commit to the holistic path and improve my health, addressing and finding strategies to manage stress had to be a priority.

I believed I could manage, but my optimism was short-lived. Seven months into my new regimen, my health took a sharp turn for the worst. I woke up one day with my left eye so blurry I could barely see, and walking up and down the stairs in my home became almost impossible. These issues signaled a severe relapse, forcing me back into the hospital for treatment.

This setback led me to a new neurologist and a pivotal conversation about my treatment options. After discussing my concerns about over-medication and side effects with this doctor, we decided on IV medication regimen every six months. This choice was significant, as it came with minimal side effects and easily integrated into my daily life. My doctor's understanding and responsiveness to my concerns were key in finding a medication that worked for me.

In addition to the medication, my comprehensive treatment strategy included stress reduction techniques, goal-setting, engaging in hobbies, and dedicating time to serving others. These activities were not merely leisurely pursuits but essential elements of my overall approach to manage my MS more effectively.

This cohesive strategy, marrying a thoughtfully chosen medication regimen with a spectrum of lifestyle adjustments, has been instrumental over the past two decades. It has allowed me to live well with MS, demonstrating that a balanced, comprehensive plan can significantly enhance health and quality of life.

Finding Equilibrium

The lesson here was clear: establishing a transparent and communicative relationship with your healthcare provider is critical. My frustration with my previous doctor stemmed from a lack of dialogue about the daily impact of my treatment's side effects, leading me to reject medical intervention entirely. However, finding a balance between medical and holistic care has been key. I've learned to manage stress, embrace a treatment plan that works for me, and maintain open lines of communication with my physician.

Now, I'm on a third of the dosage I started with, thanks to my body's positive response to the treatment, and I remain relapse-free. Now I understand the importance of a comprehensive approach to managing MS, one that includes medication when necessary but also emphasizes lifestyle, mental health, and personal well-being.

Steps To a Balanced Treatment Plan

Creating a balanced treatment plan for Multiple Sclerosis (MS) involves an approach that extends beyond conventional medical treatments to include lifestyle and mental health considerations. The key steps to achieving this balance include fostering open communication with your healthcare provider, educating yourself about your condition, making lifestyle adjustments, prioritizing mental health, seeking community support, and embracing your personal health. This holistic strategy empowers you to take an active role in managing your MS, ensuring that your treatment plan supports not just your physical health but your overall well-being, leading to a more fulfilling life despite the challenges of the condition.

Open Dialogue with Your Doctor

Establish a relationship with your healthcare provider based on open communication. Feel empowered to ask questions and express your preferences. This partnership is crucial for navigating your treatment options effectively.

Personal Research

Educate yourself about your condition and the available treatments. Knowledge is power, and understanding your options will help you make informed decisions about your care.

Lifestyle Adjustments
Incorporate changes into your daily life that support your overall well-being. This can include dietary modifications, regular exercise, and mindfulness practices. These adjustments can complement your medical treatments and enhance your quality of life.

Mental Health
Recognize the impact of your mental health on your physical well-being. Seek support through counseling or therapy to manage stress, anxiety, or depression that can accompany chronic illness.

Community and Support
Engage with support groups, either in person or online. Connecting with others who are navigating similar paths can provide comfort, insight, and motivation.

Embracing Your Journey
My experience with MS treatment has taught me the value of being an active participant in my healthcare decisions. It's about more than just following the doctor's orders; it's about crafting a life that supports your health on all levels. This empowerment has led me to a place of balance and peace, demonstrating the power of a comprehensive approach to health.

Remember, treatment for MS or any chronic condition is a deeply personal experience. It requires a blend of medical intervention, lifestyle choices, and mental health support. By taking proactive steps and engaging in open dialogue with your healthcare team, you can craft a treatment plan that supports your overall well-being and leads to a fulfilling life despite the challenges of MS.

Walk Away from the Game

After settling into a health plan that was balanced and beneficial for me, I was inspired to write a poem that captured the essence of my struggle and subsequent empowerment in managing Multiple Sclerosis (MS). This wasn't just any piece of writing; it was a narrative that transformed my battle with medications and treatments into a metaphorical baseball game, illustrating the trials and triumphs of becoming an active participant in my care.

The poem depicts me as the batter, with doctors as my coaches advising me to trust their game plan to stay ahead of MS. As I stepped up to the plate with my eyes closed, expected to swing perfectly, symbolizes the attempt to halt the disease's progression without acknowledging that there were actionable steps I could partake in—like incorporating a positive mindset, stress management, better nutrition, exercise, and setting goals—that could contribute to the improvement of my condition. This narrative of empowerment illuminated the realization that, despite being unwillingly cast into the game of MS, I wielded the power to affect its direction. This act of writing allowed me to express that I was far from a passive participant in my healthcare; rather, I was the key player with the autonomy to influence my treatment decisions. This moment of clarity in the poem was pivotal, signifying my shift to taking an active stance in managing my condition, prompting me to question, research, and implement lifestyle changes that markedly improved my mind and physical health.

While I know I do not have control over MS, I have the power to influence how I manage it and its impact on my life. I possess the authority to shape how I think about the disease and have influence over it by using my "Secret Sauce" that I had indicated in this book. This poem highlights my transition from feeling overwhelmed to being empowered. It was a declaration of my commitment to a balanced approach to managing MS, and a celebration of regaining my power in a situation that once felt overwhelmingly powerless.

Walk Away from the Game
A poem by Ashley Ivey

What if
Multiple Sclerosis did not have to be progressive,
The diagnosis did not define your future,
The definition did not lack your input?
What if
2004 could have played out differently?
If I could have opted out of the game like a child with options?
But
My options were not known, they were not shown
Or spoken of.
Stuck in a sport I wanted no part of.
But like a child, I learned to cope and embrace the sport I was picked for.
I grew and knew the plays, pauses, and losses.
I get used to – no, I expect them.
I learned to use the sport, to be the sport, to love the sport.
Because it's all I know.
With crowds around chanting,
This is the place for me,
That, yes, this is who you are.
How do you tell them to not pick the outcome before you are up to bat?
To stop cheering when you lose?
You were supposed to want me to win!
Stepping to the plate,
Conflicted.
Its dark.
My
Weighted eyes closed.
Because that is how I was taught to play the game.
Close my eyes, dispose my thoughts, and listen to coach.
Being afraid secured my loss, but
Coach taught me to live in fear.
 Location of ball unknown,
 So
 How do I hit it if I can see?
See, he tells me to take the chance at what he does with my eyes closed.
Will help prevent the ball from striking,
But it hits me every time.
Coach said I lost this game,
But he made me continue to play it.
Not telling me that I have options,

That
Long ago,
I could have said no!
The he could have shown me ways
To win every game,
No matter the opposing team, or the heat of the day, or the stress I am under.
Showed me ways to take ownership over my win,
To expect my win,
And never know the definition of a loss.
What If
I opened my eyes, see the clear skies
And the fans,
Cheering!
Reality.
See, that this game has an ending I can change.
I see coach, with pockets full of green.
Money given by the referees to ensure my loss.
Too much at stake with my Victory!
Oh I see, Praise God for vision to See!
Use me Lord to teach this team their options.
Allow me to show them
That despite getting picked for this game,
How to play with eyes wide open,
How to never get hit by the ball
To redefine the game and walk away from it.
Because as I speak,
I sit outside the arena
Warm with knowledge and truth
Trying to save those still inside.
I tell them,
You have influence over this game,
The diagnosis did not define your future, because the definition included your input.
Walk away from the game.

Chapter 11

Secret Sauce #4
Having an advocate
Someone to speak for you when you cannot.

Merriam-Webster's dictionary defines an advocate as:
1. One who defends or maintains a cause or proposal.
2. One who supports or promotes the interests of a cause or group.

When you're ill, the overwhelming challenge of managing your healthcare, including dealing with insurance and following up with doctors, means you're not in the best position to make objective decisions or carry out the necessary tasks needed to ensure your well-being. This is precisely why having an advocate is so crucial. An advocate serves as your voice and your champion, navigating the healthcare system on your behalf when you're least able to do so. They understand the intricacies of medical jargon, insurance policies, and treatment options, enabling them to make informed, objective decisions and communicate effectively with medical professionals. Their role is to ensure that your needs are met, your rights are protected, and you receive the best possible care without the added stress of managing it all by yourself, highlighting the vital importance of advocacy in healthcare.

My mom has been my unwavering advocate since my initial diagnosis with multiple sclerosis (MS). She took up my cause with a determination that ensured not just my survival, but my ability to thrive despite the prognosis. To this day, doctors acknowledge that my current state of health—walking and being able to do things independently—is largely due to her advocacy, her meticulous research, and her proactive approach in managing my care. When initial treatments, like steroid pills, failed to stop my decline, she recognized the urgency, pushing doctors to hospitalize me for IV steroids to speed up the recovery from an MS relapse. She knew that minimizing the duration of inflammation in my brain and spinal cord was crucial to reduce the risk of permanent damage.

Her active involvement in my healthcare was unmistakable. All my doctors had her contact information, ensuring she was always up to date on my condition. Her presence was a constant reminder to the medical staff that I had someone looking out for me, leading to noticeably better care. Whether in the hospital, school, or any other care setting, knowing that a patient has someone advocating for them can significantly improve the quality of care they receive.

My mother's dedication extended to ensuring I received the best possible treatment. Armed with comprehensive medical records she didn't hesitate to demand attention from the top specialists at Johns Hopkins, despite not having an appointment. Her efforts paid off when the head of the MS center acknowledged the severity of my condition and initiated an aggressive treatment plan that included chemotherapy and plasmapheresis to squelch the MS relapse I was going through.

Beyond medical treatments, her savvy in navigating insurance and medical benefits was a lifeline. She successfully petitioned for me to receive Medicare at 19, leveraging my previous work history to secure coverage more comprehensive than Medicaid would have offered. This foresight, paired with her securing coverage under my parents' insurance through an incapacitation determination, meant I had unparalleled access to specialists, treatments, and medications.

Having an advocate is more than just having support; it's about having someone who can navigate the complex medical and insurance systems, advocate for aggressive treatments, and ensure the patient's needs are met with urgency and care. My mother's role as my advocate was instrumental in improving my health, highlighting the profound impact that knowledgeable, dedicated advocacy can have on a patient's care and outcome.

Positive People

Having an advocate is crucial when facing illness or injury, but surrounding yourself with positive people is equally beneficial. Positivity acts like a healing balm, accelerating the recovery process and infusing you with hope and strength. For me, my mother was not only my advocate but also a beacon of positivity throughout my MS journey. Not once did I hear her express doubt or fear about my condition; instead, she radiated unwavering belief in my ability to overcome challenges. Similarly, my father's constant reassurances during the toughest times instilled in me a sense of optimism and resilience. Beyond my immediate family, friends and church members offered words of encouragement and scriptures that uplifted my spirits during MS relapses and difficult moments. Surrounding yourself with positive-minded individuals is essential because we absorb the energy of those closest to us. However, finding positivity isn't always easy, especially when loved ones may not be in the right space to offer it. In such cases, it's okay to create some mental distance to protect your well-being. As my childhood pastor used to say, "It's okay to love from afar, with a long-handled spoon." Negativity can drain our energy, affecting both our minds and bodies. Have you ever felt exhausted after being around someone who is constantly negative? I certainly have, which is why I prioritize surrounding myself with positivity. If you need more positive influences in your life, consider engaging with uplifting podcasts or motivational videos to fill your mind with thoughts of hope. Personally, I'm intentional about what I allow into my mind, whether it's people's opinions, social media content, or TV programs, ensuring everything uplifts and encourages me throughout the day. Positivity isn't just a mindset; it's a powerful tool that shapes how we navigate life's challenges, including illness.

Chapter 12

Secret Sauce #5
Faith, the Unseen Anchor in My Journey

Growing up in a church environment, I was imbued with stories of faith and divine guidance from a young age. Yet, the true depth of these teachings only struck me after the significant MS relapse in my late 20s, following my decision to halt all medical interventions. It was a critical juncture; I recognized that placing my trust solely in doctors was futile—they couldn't possibly know everything. Similarly, I realized my self-reliance alone was faltering, overwhelmed by stress from factors beyond my control.

This crisis brought me to a pivotal realization: true faith means fully surrendering to Christ, embracing His plan which far exceeds my understanding and fears. It instilled in me a sense of humility and hope, teaching me to entrust all my concerns to Him and to believe wholeheartedly in the path He has set for me. What truly amazes me is the realization that I'm placing my trust in a God who has the power to address my issues. This isn't about blind faith in an indifferent force; it's about believing in God who is both willing and capable of making a difference in my life. Faith in Christ involves letting go of our worries and believing in His guiding hand. It's about knowing His love is steadfast and He wants only what's best for us. This faith helps us see that our trials are not without purpose—they're designed to promote growth, encourage change, or prepare us to inspire and help others.

> Jeremiah 29:11 "For I know the plans I have for you, declares the Lord, plans to prosper you and not to harm you, plans to give you hope and a future."

Clinging to this promise, I entrust my path to Christ, believing He holds the ultimate blueprint of my life.

MS Relapse, My Faith & My Right Hand

> 2 Corinthians 12:9: But he said to me, my grace is sufficient for you, for my power is made perfect in weakness. Therefore, I will boast all the more gladly of my weaknesses, so that the power of Christ may rest upon me.

At the age of 28, I experienced another relapse. Until then, my recoveries from relapses had been relatively swift, usually taking just a few weeks for my mobility, vision, speech, or sensation to begin improving. I had been fortunate to avoid any permanent damage or lasting symptoms from previous episodes. However, this time was different; the recovery process was markedly slower. Living alone while my parents vacationed in Florida, I chose to keep the situation to myself. Having become accustomed to quick recoveries, I had almost come to expect God's intervention in restoring my health as a given. But this relapse at age 28 challenged my perspective, prompting me to question, "Ash, can you maintain your faith and positivity even if recovery doesn't come as swiftly as before?"

Struggling to climb the stairs in my own house became my new reality. Driving was a gamble, with a persistent black spot marring my vision, and relying solely on my car's sensors to alert me of other vehicles lurking in my blind spots. My legs would suddenly fail me, and my right hand became unresponsive, devoid of movement or sensation. The question haunted me, "How could this be happening again?" A decade had passed since my MS diagnosis—a decade that marked both triumph and trial. I had reached a point where multiple doctors had ominously predicted, where moving independently without the aid of a wheelchair, cane, or walker seemed almost unfeasible. Admitting I needed help was a battle; a confrontation with my vulnerability I wasn't ready to face. Denial became a flimsy shield against the glaring truth of my condition, making the acceptance of my physical limitations an even steeper climb.

I completely lost feeling in my right arm and hand, which I normally use for everything. It felt like they weren't even part of me anymore. I couldn't get them to do anything I wanted; my arm just hung there, and my hand couldn't feel a thing. This meant I couldn't grasp or hold onto objects—everything I tried to pick up might as well have been made of air. All the things I used to do easily, like writing, tying my shoes, cooking, doing my hair, or even just closing a door, became impossible. Even when I touched my face with my right hand, it felt like someone else's hand, not mine.

I realized that accepting help wasn't a sign of weakness but beneficial for me. I gathered the courage to inform my parents about my relapse, and they were understandably concerned. My doctor quickly arranged for me to undergo various treatments at the hospital, including a mix of familiar and new approaches. I went through physical and occupational therapy to regain my ability to walk, and doctors prescribed steroids to lessen the inflammation in my optic nerve, which helped improve my vision gradually.

Despite these improvements, we encountered a standstill with restoring feeling or movement in my right arm and hand. The medical team tried a variety of further treatments and medications for several weeks, yet we saw no improvement.

The hospital's final verdict was a heavy blow; there was nothing more they could do to restore strength or sensation to my arm and hand. Their efforts had reached their limit, and with that, they sent me home

After getting out of the hospital, I had to move in with my parents because my own place, with its stairs, just wasn't feasible at this point. This is where I started to really lean on my faith. I stumbled upon this song, "Amen" by Deitrick Haddon, which hit home for me, especially because it kicked off with the verse from Roman s 8:18 "For I Reckon that the sufferings of this present time are not worthy to be compared with the glory that shall be revealed in us". I must've listened to that song hundreds of times. It was a tough time—it felt like everyone, doctors included, had pretty much written me off. But that song, that verse, gave me hope. It made me believe that no matter how tough things were now, there was something much better ahead that God had planned for me.

Even though the doctors didn't see a way forward, I couldn't just give up. We tried to find a physical therapist who could help but hit another roadblock when we found out they didn't have anyone experienced with my kind of issues. That was frustrating, but it didn't stop me. When we got back to my parents' place, I told my mom that I wasn't going to wait around for someone else to fix this. I had to keep at it, believing that with faith in Christ, I'd get through this new challenge. It became more than just trying to get better physically; it was about proving to myself that with enough faith and determination, I could face anything. The scripture Romans 8:18 "For I reckon that the sufferings of this present time are not worthy to be compared with the glory that shall be revealed in us". continued to echo in my mind as I asked my parents to let me go home and try to navigate healing in my own space.

My parents decided to get some extra help for me by hiring a caregiver from our company, and though I was initially embarrassed about needing assistance, it turned out to be a great decision. Esther, the caregiver who came to my house, was incredible. She helped me with everything—from cooking tacos and bathing to navigating the stairs in my house. She even drove me to my doctor appointments and MRI scans. When it was just the two of us, she'd chat with me, sing, and even style my hair. Having her around made a huge difference during a really difficult time; it was reassuring to have someone we trusted by my side.

As I began to recover, my right hand still wasn't back to normal; I couldn't feel anything with it. Despite the seeming lack of hope from doctors and therapists, I wasn't ready to give up on myself. I made a conscious choice to keep using my right hand, repeatedly forcing myself to engage it in activities. One strategy I came up with was practicing turning off the shower water with my right hand. Initially, I had to use my left hand to position my right hand on the knob. Then, I'd attempt to move it, first with some help from my left and then trying with just my right. To add to the challenge, after finishing my shower, I'd turn the water cold with my left hand, forcing myself to use my right hand to turn it off or else face a freezing shower. This became my routine for months.

Below is a poem I wrote about this journey, titled "Tears."

Tears

A Poem by Ashley Ivey

Cold,
Water dripping,
I
Try,
But try is not enough.
I
Look,

But looking does no good,
Cause I can't look and make my hand
Work at all, the way it should.

Disappointed, I stood,

Wet.
Cold.
Dreaming of good things.
Praying, thinking, and listening.
Water from the shower glistening.

My tears make noise.

Warm tears, heat, the cold water around me.
My faith implored action.
I knew that was the key.

Using my left hand, I
placed my right hand on the shower handle,

Left hand squeezing right hand on the metal.
I was going to turn this water off, no room to settle.

Left hand assisting the right,
I cried as I held on tight.
I looked and told my hand to move.
It was limp, but I had faith it would improve.

Slowly, my hands turned the knob.
My body cold as I sobbed.

"Lord, let's do this!"
I exclaimed,
"Faith without works is nothing," I proclaimed!
Each morning this was my shower routine.
Forcing use of my right hand to get clean.
Turn the water on with my left hand, but turn it off, use the right.
Slowly, but surely, each try gave me more fight.
This hand will work, and I believe.
The Lord is with me, and He will never leave.
Many cold showers I had, as it took awhile.
But slowly my tears turned into a smile.
I could feel the cold with my right hand.
I could turn and twist and move as planned.
Perseverance in faith,
Trying and forcing through,
Thank you, Lord, for making this hand anew.

To regain full use, it took two years,
Hard work,
My faith,
Now I cry thankful tears.

Deeply rooted in faith, my unwavering trust in the Lord and the support of those around me provided the foundation I needed during my darkest hours. Even when the path to recovery seemed uncertain, my faith was the beacon of light that guided me. I held onto the belief that faith in Christ was not just about enduring trials but about taking decisive action in the face of adversity. This conviction propelled me to believe in the possibility of recovery and actively pursue it. My faith taught me not to passively await change but to engage with my challenges head-on, embodying the essence of faith in action.

The doubts cast by others on my capacity to heal only strengthened my resolve. I was comforted by the knowledge that Christ was with me, drawing parallels between my struggles and His sacrifices. This comparison was not about equating my experiences to His but about drawing strength from His example of resilience and unwavering faith under the most grueling circumstances. This profound connection to Christ's journey gave me the courage to face my own challenges, reinforcing my belief that if He could endure, so could I.

At the time, I had no idea that the resilience built from my faith and actions during my health struggles would serve a profound purpose beyond my own recovery. It fascinatingly prepared me for a critical challenge nearly a decade later when my son faced his own health crisis. This experience was a powerful testament to the enduring strength of faith and its ability to guide us through life's most unexpected trials.

The Cycle of Faith & Advocacy Continues

My daughter's name is Angela. She is 6 and a half years old. My son's name is Kevin and he is 4 and a half years old. When Angela was born, she had a tiny face and a lot of hair, so I started calling her Bookie Bear. As for my son, I always tell him that he has the cutest little boy face I have ever seen in my whole life, so I call him "Cute Face Kevin."

In September of 2023, I had a conflict in my schedule and asked my mom to take both my children to their annual pediatrician office visit for a physical. She called me after the visit and told me about what the doctor reported- Angie was in 97% for height for her age, and Kevin was in the 99th percentile for height for his age. I am five foot nine inches, so it was no surprise to me that their heights were off the charts. They both had great exams, they exceeded tests and were thriving well. However, there was concern about something the doctor saw on my son's eye exam.

Vision

A Poem by Ashley Ivey

It was a routine visit to the pediatrician,
Where they discovered something missing in my 4-year old's vision.
An absent red reflex in his beautiful left eye,
They referred us to a specialist to figure out why.
From that specialist to a surgeon
We were referred right away,
The news was devastating is the least I can say.
I said
Let's try John Hopkins!
The best that I knew
Called at 9, appointment at 11
And away we flew.
He saw two specialists that very same day
That looked in his eye, did tests as I prayed
They said he can't see
His retina doesn't look right
My baby couldn't see images, all he could see was light.
They described a cataract that is occluding his vision
A vitreous hemorrhage had occurred
Surgery, their final decision.
I cried and I cried
I wanted to shut both my ears
Take my Kev, hug him tight
And disregard all my fears
I looked into his eyes
And all I saw was perfection
"Cute face Kevin" I call him
How was there need for correction?
I sat and I prayed
 And thanked God for my son
I cried and I asked for God's will to be done.
Peace filled my lungs
Gratefulness filled my heart with joy.
I have faith that God will provide for my cute face little boy.
I praised the Lord in advance,
For the miracles on the way.
He reminds me of the healing,
He does each and every day.

When I got the initial news of my son's diagnosis, I wanted to just take him, run to a corner, hold him and never let him go. I wanted to cancel everything, all my meetings, appointments, a spiritual retreat in which I was one of the speakers. The Holy Spirit whispered to me to push harder not to do this. To not insulate and isolate myself in this issue. And to continue life- one step at a time. But I didn't want to go anywhere-including church. At church, someone would inevitably ask me how I was doing. At church, I had to confront God and ask Him- Why Kevin? Why this? But the Church is exactly where God led me.

In my feelings of despair about Kevin's eye, I went to the body of Christ, the church, and inevitably poured out my sadness. The church was gentle with me, prayed with me, consoled me and encouraged me to think differently about this situation; to see the Lord working in every situation, regardless of whether I felt it was good or bad. That is why I believe the Lord wants us to stay with the church during good and bad times.

Have you ever wanted to go into isolation when something tragic happens in your life? Have you felt like no one would understand? I've been there and I am glad the spirit insisted for me to say no to isolation and say yes to His people.

The Holy Spirit continued to push me to go further, to do more despite my sadness and fear about Kevin's lack of vision in his left eye. I went to a church small group session and received an unexpected gift. A long-time friend who attended the small group gave a testimony that spoke to me. It was as if the Holy Spirit told him exactly what to say (Go figure!). The testimony reminded me that God is faithful, and that I have people and witnesses around me that have gone through tragic, tough times, but continued life- pushed through the pain and trusted in the Lord.

He told us about a couple from his church whose daughter was facing a significant health challenge. Despite the uncertainty of their situation, this couple's response was remarkable for their steadfastness and faith. He observed how they continued to pray, stayed connected with their church community, and supported one another through the ordeal. He was particularly moved by how, despite the difficult circumstances, this family's resilience and trust in God not only sustained them but also led to their daughter's significant health improvement. This story, as recounted by Jonathan, served as a profound inspiration to me, highlighting the power of faith, trust in the Lord and how your faith can inspire others to have faith during trying times.

Right there in that small group, Jonathan was a bridge reminding me of God's goodness and Grace. He stood in that gap for me, when my disappointment blinded me from the fact that the Lord is Sovereign, and He is a healer.

After Kevin's diagnosis, the Holy Spirit continued to push me further into connection and told me to commune with Him directly. One morning, while walking on the treadmill, I watched a sermon in which the pastor was teaching from the book Isaiah. In that sermon he showed how we "God's people" quickly forget the grace and the power of God when going through a tough situation. I was convicted. I realized that my son's diagnosis was not the only diagnosis I have dealt with. There I stood, 19 years after my MS diagnosis, a witness to God's faithfulness.

Kevin's diagnosis is not the first diagnosis the Lord has dealt with. You see, in that small group, when our longtime friend testified about watching a family in the church go through tough times with their sick daughter, he was recounting the story of my own family—my parents were the resilient souls he admired. I was the child facing those significant health challenges he mentioned. He spoke about observing my parents navigate the turbulent waters of my MS diagnosis. Despite frequent hospitalizations and daunting prognoses, their faith in God never wavered. They remained steadfast in their church attendance, love for Christ, and praise for His goodness. Two decades had nearly passed, yet the example of faith my parents set continues to inspire Jonathan and others in our community.

God's foresight in preparing me for my son Kevin's journey was a clear demonstration of His providential care. He knew the trials we would face and equipped me with a deep faith forged through my own battle with health challenges. This wasn't just preparation for me but also for Kevin, ensuring that he was born into a family that understood perseverance, hope, and the power of prayer.

Faced with Kevin's diagnosis, my prayer life deepened and evolved. Initially, my prayers centered on seeking total healing for his eye, but with encouragement from my church family, they shifted towards a surrender to God's will regardless of the outcome. This was a profound and challenging transformation, yet it brought an unparalleled peace and acceptance of God's plan for Kevin's life. It removed the burden of guilt from my shoulders and reinforced my trust in God's loving care for my son.

The miraculous turn of events following Kevin's surgeries was nothing short of divine intervention. At a doctor's appointment after the second eye surgery, his surgeon was amazed to see his retina not only intact but in great condition! Weeks before, this doctor and several others stated and showed us evidence that Kevin's retina had been destroyed, which they assumed was from a traumatic injury to his eye. They were preparing us for life with Kevin only seeing from one eye. We learned post-second surgery that Kevin had not had a traumatic event but a congenital "malformation" that caused the total cataract and issue with his retina. However, they did not know how the retina appeared when they previously thought it was destroyed. Kevin can see out of his left eye. He can see.

I also do not believe it was a "malformation" as they described. God made Kevin's eye perfect and with purpose. Kevin's life may be challenged because he sees life differently due to a slight reduction in his visual field in the left eye, but I am sure, Kevin will find purpose in pain, strength in his struggle, and understand the incredible power he possesses to live life despite adversity.

I tell him all the time that I have never known anyone who has had three eye surgeries at the age of 5, and that God is making him strong. At a young age, God is preparing him to do something wonderful, to witness something great, and to share his story with others. Highlighting the ability to endure significant medical challenges at such a young age, I'm sending a message that God's love is molding him for a unique purpose. Kevin's challenge and the strength he's developing will inspire and benefit others. I want him to view adversity as I do, as preparation. Preparation for something extraordinary in the future, providing an opportunity to share the positive outcomes of his experiences and to give the gift of hope.

This miracle was a testament to God's grace and the power of faith. Kevin's path to regaining vision is a lesson in patience, rehabilitation, and gradual improvement, but it's a path we walk with hope and gratitude.

Faith is not essential in things that are easy; its true test arises in moments of difficulty or uncertainty. This experience has not only continued to strengthen my faith but has also shown me the purpose behind my own struggles with Multiple Sclerosis. It prepared me to be Kevin's strongest advocate, using all the tools I learned from my mother's advocacy for me. I am profoundly thankful for the support of our church community and for the opportunity to bear witness to God's unfailing love and healing power.

Faith is the single most important part of my Secret Sauce. Our story is a testament to the strength that comes from faith, the miracles that unfold from trust, and the peace that prevails through surrender. It reaffirms the truth that in every challenge lies an opportunity to witness the boundless grace of God. As I share our journey, I do so with a heart full of gratitude, knowing that our lives are a living testimony to the scripture that continues to be my anchor:

> Romans 8:18, "For I reckon that the sufferings of this present time are not worthy to be compared with the glory which shall be revealed in us."

Thank you for taking this journey with me and learning Why I-CARE Too.

ABOUT THE AUTHORS

Donna Ivey embarked on her remarkable journey into healthcare at 14, laying the foundation for her to become a prominent figure in her community's healthcare landscape. After starting her path as a pre-med chemistry student, Donna gained practical healthcare experience working with a group of neurologists before completing her degree in Business. In 1993, she founded I-CARE Inc., a home healthcare company renowned for its excellence in caring for clients of all ages. In addition to her professional work, Donna became an advocate not only for her patients but also for her daughter, Ashley, who was diagnosed with MS at 18. In this book, Donna shares insights on transitioning from family caregiver to advocate, offering practical guidance and relatable case studies for those navigating similar paths.

Ashley Ivey's introduction to the healthcare world also began at a young age, working alongside her parents at I-CARE. Celebrating her 14th birthday with a worker's permit and a birthday cake, Ashley was the first of the three Ivey children to be incorporated into the family company at the age of 14. However, her life took an unforeseen turn with a diagnosis of Multiple Sclerosis at 18. Despite the initial prognosis predicting confinement to a wheelchair within 10 years, by the grace of God, Ashley not only walks but strides confidently in heels. Two decades later, she shares her "secret sauce"—the strategies and wisdom cultivated over years of resilience—to empower others facing similar hurdles. Through her heartfelt poetry and personal reflections, Ashley illuminates a path of self-discovery and strength despite obstacles.

Made in the USA
Middletown, DE
17 April 2024